1st Workshop on Benchmarking: Past, Present and Future (BPPF 2021)

Bangkok, Thailand and Online
5-6 August 2021

ISBN: 978-1-7138-9159-8

Printed from e-media with permission by:

Curran Associates, Inc.
57 Morehouse Lane
Red Hook, NY 12571

Some format issues inherent in the e-media version may also appear in this print version.

Printed with permission by Curran Associates, Inc. (2024)

Association for Computational Linguistics
209 N. Eighth Street
Stroudsburg, Pennsylvania 18360

Phone: 1-570-476-8006
Fax: 1-570-476-0860

acl@aclweb.org

Additional copies of this publication are available from:

Curran Associates, Inc.
57 Morehouse Lane
Red Hook, NY 12571 USA
Phone: 845-758-0400
Fax: 845-758-2633
Email: curran@proceedings.com
Web: www.proceedings.com

BPPF 2021

The 1st Workshop on Benchmarking: Past, Present and Future

Proceedings of the Workshop

August 5–6, 2021
Bangkok, Thailand (online)

Message from the Program Chairs

Where have we been, and where are we going? It is easier to talk about the past than the future. These days, benchmarks evolve more bottom up (such as papers with code). There used to be more top-down leadership from government (and industry, in the case of systems, with benchmarks such as SPEC). Going forward, there may be more top-down leadership from organizations like MLPerf and/or influencers like David Ferrucci, who was responsible for IBM's success with Jeopardy, and has recently written a paper suggesting how the community should think about benchmarking for machine comprehension. Tasks such as reading comprehension become even more interesting as we move beyond English. Multilinguality introduces many challenges, and even more opportunities.

Organizing Committee

Workshop Organizers:

Kenneth Church (Baidu, USA)
Mark Liberman (Penn, USA)
Valia Kordoni (Humboldt, Germany)

Program Committee:

Eduardo Blanco (University of North Texas)
Nicoletta Calzolari (Italy)
Kenneth Church (Baidu, USA)
Christian Federmann (Microsoft Research, USA)
Valia Kordoni (Humboldt, Germany)
Julia Hirshberg (Columbia, USA)
Lori Lamel (LIMSI, France)
Mark Liberman (Penn, USA)
Phillip Koehn (JHU, USA)
Barbara Plank (IT University of Copenhagen, Denmark)
Preslav Nakov (Qatar Computing Research Institute (QCRI), HBKU)
Anette Frank (University of Heidelberg, Germany)
Roy Bar-Haim (IBM Research - Haifa, Israel)

Table of Contents

Conference Program

Benchmarking: Past, Present and Future

Kenneth Church
Baidu, CA, USA

Mark Liberman
University of Pennsylvania, PA, USA

Valia Kordoni
Humboldt-Universitaet zu Berlin, Germany

Abstract

Where have we been, and where are we going? It is easier to talk about the past than the future. These days, benchmarks evolve more bottom up (such as papers with code).[1] There used to be more top-down leadership from government (and industry, in the case of systems, with benchmarks such as SPEC).[2] Going forward, there may be more top-down leadership from organizations like MLPerf[3] and/or influencers like David Ferrucci[4]. Tasks such as reading comprehension become even more interesting as we move beyond English. Multilinguality introduces many challenges, and even more opportunities.

1 Abstracts for Invited Talks

We have an amazing collection of invited speakers that can share with us first hand knowledge of how benchmarking became important in Information Retrieval, and then in speech (starting around 1975), and then in language (in 1988). Much of this history is described in this video[6] and two 2016 Interspeech keynotes: Makhoul describes how benchmarking overcame resistance in speech in this keynote,[7] and Jurafsky describes how this approach moved from speech to language in this keynote.[8]

Web site for workshop is here[9]

1.1 What Will it Take to Fix Benchmarking in Natural Language Understanding?

Sam Bowman
New York University
https://cims.nyu.edu/~sbowman/
https://twitter.com/sleepinyourhat

Evaluation for many natural language understanding (NLU) tasks is broken: Unreliable and biased systems score so highly on standard benchmarks that there is little room for researchers who develop better systems to demonstrate their improvements. The recent trend to abandon IID benchmarks in favor of adversarially-constructed, out-of-distribution test sets ensures that current models will perform poorly, but ultimately only obscures the abilities that we want our benchmarks to measure. In this position paper, we lay out four criteria that we argue NLU benchmarks should meet. We argue most current benchmarks fail at these criteria, and that adversarial data collection does not meaningfully address the causes of these failures. Instead, restoring a healthy evaluation ecosystem will require significant progress in the design of benchmark datasets, the reliability with which they are annotated, their size, and the ways they handle social bias.

1.1.1 Bio

Sam Bowman has been on the faculty at NYU since 2016, when he completed PhD with Chris Manning and Chris Potts at Stanford. At NYU, he is a member of the Center for Data Science, the Department of Linguistics, and Courant Institute's Department of Computer Science. His research focuses on data, evaluation techniques, and modeling techniques for sentence and paragraph

[1] https://paperswithcode.com/
[2] https://www.spec.org/benchmarks.html
[3] https://mlperf.org/
[4] https://en.wikipedia.org/wiki/David_Ferrucci, who was responsible for IBM's success with Jeopardy,[5] and has recently written a paper suggesting how the community should think about benchmarking for machine comprehension (Dunietz et al., 2020)
[6] https://www.simonsfoundation.org/search/liberman/
[7] https://www.superlectures.com/interspeech2016/isca-medalist-for-leadership-and-extensive-contributions-to-speech-and-language-processing
[8] https://www.superlectures.com/interspeech2016/ketchup-interdisciplinarity-and-the-spread-of-innovation-in-speech-and-language-processing
[9] https://github.com/kwchurch/Benchmarking_past_present_future

Proceedings of the 1st Workshop on Benchmarking: Past, Present and Future, pages 1–7
August 5–6, 2021.

understanding in natural language processing, and on applications of machine learning to scientific questions in linguistic syntax and semantics. He is the senior organizer behind the GLUE and SuperGLUE benchmark competitions; he organized a twenty-three-person research team at JSALT 2018; and he received a 2015 EMNLP Best Resource Paper Award, a 2019 *SEM Best Paper Award, and a 2017 Google Faculty Research Award.

1.2 Context for Interpreting Benchmark Performances

Eunsol Choi

Interpreting benchmark results requires a more nuanced study than simply comparing a single number (e.g., accuracy). For example, higher performance on benchmark focusing on multi-hop reasoning does not translate to model architecture focusing on multi-hop reasoning but often a bigger pretrained model. In the first half of the talk, I will discuss the nuances of interpreting benchmark results, and our previous efforts in integrating highly relevant axis, computational resources, into evaluation. In the second half of the talk, I will talk about the issues with the static benchmarks in the evolving world. Unlike traditional benchmarks which mostly targeted linguistic knowledge, modern benchmark embraces common sense, social context, and encyclopedic world knowledge into the task definition. All these components change over time, urging NLP benchmarks to be refreshed.

1.2.1 Bio

Eunsol Choi is an assistant professor in the computer science department at the University of Texas at Austin. Her research focuses on natural language processing, various ways to recover semantics from unstructured text. Prior to UT, she was a visiting faculty researcher at Google AI. She received a Ph.D. from the University of Washington (with Luke Zettlemoyer and Yejin Choi) and an undergraduate degree in mathematics and computer science from Cornell University. She is a recipient Facebook Research Fellowship, Google Research Award and has co-organized many workshops related to question answering at NLP and ML venues.

1.3 Moving out of the comfort zones: desired shifts in NLP benchmarking

Ido Dagan
Bar-Ilan University
`https://u.cs.biu.ac.il/~dagan/`

As the deep-learning era has transformed the NLP field, benchmarking practices haven't changed that much, often addressing earlier language analysis tasks and applications. While performance on many benchmarks rocketed, mostly in deep learning comfort zones, profound language technology is still a long way ahead. In this talk, I will argue for three desired interrelated shifts in NLP benchmarking, which motivate and support each other, that should direct further research.

First, much more emphasis should be given to typical realistic settings, in which large training data for the target task is not available, like few-shot and transfer learning. Moreover, benchmarks design should fit realistic data compositions, rather than synthetic ones within the comfort zone, as I will illustrate by a recent few-shot relation classification dataset. Second, recognizing the limits of foreseeable fully-automated methods in addressing the hard NLP challenges, I suggest developing principled evaluation methodologies for various interactive NLP settings. Interaction may lead to better results, with the help of a human in the loop, and moreover allow personalized and explorative behavior, as I will demonstrate with a recent framework for evaluating interactive summarization. Lastly, while many current models operate in an end-to-end manner over implicit language structures, I argue that it is pertinent to pursue also explicit representations for textual information structure, to facilitate refined and better-controlled modeling. Unlike traditional semantic formalisms, I propose pursuing semi-structured representations, consisting of natural language expressions over which current powerful text-embeddings can be applied. I will illustrate this direction by an approach for decomposing the information in single and multiple texts into sets of question-answer pairs, and draw some analogies from our successful experience in designing the Recognizing Textual Entailment (RTE, later aka NLI) task.

1.3.1 Bio

Ido Dagan is a Professor at the Department of Computer Science at Bar-Ilan University, Israel, the founder of the Natural Language Processing (NLP) Lab at Bar-Ilan, the founder and head of the nationally-funded Bar-Ilan University Data Science Institute and a Fellow of the Association for Computational Linguistics (ACL). His interests are in applied semantic processing, focusing on textual inference, natural open semantic representations, consolidation and summarization of multi-text information, and interactive text summarization. Dagan and colleagues initiated textual entailment recognition (RTE, later aka NLI) as a generic empirical task. He was the President of the ACL in 2010 and served on its Executive Committee during 2008-2011. In that capacity, he led the establishment of the journal Transactions of the Association for Computational Linguistics, which became one of two premiere journals in NLP. Dagan received his B.A. summa cum laude and his Ph.D. (1992) in Computer Science from the Technion. He was a research fellow at the IBM Haifa Scientific Center (1991) and a Member of Technical Staff at AT&T Bell Laboratories (1992-1994). During 1998-2003 he was co-founder and CTO of FocusEngine and VP of Technology of LingoMotors, and has been regularly consulting in the industry. His academic research has involved extensive industrial collaboration, including funds from IBM, Google, Thomson-Reuters, Bloomberg, Intel and Facebook, as well as collaboration with local companies under funded projects of the Israel Innovation Authority.

1.4 MLPerf

Greg Diamos, Peter Mattson and **David Kanter**
https://www.anandtech.com/show/14754/hot-chips-31-live-blogs-mlperf-benchmark

Two topics: (1) What is MLPerf? (2) Advice for groups wanting to create new sets of benchmarks.

1.4.1 Bio

Greg is helping build Landing AI, a new company focused on bringing AI to every major industry starting with our first manufacturing visual inspection product, LandingLens. Greg co-founded MLPerf and MLCommons. Greg helped found Baidu's Silicon Valley AI Lab, where he contributed to the DeepSpeech, DeepVoice, and Mixed Precision training systems. Greg contributed the independent thread scheduling system to the NVIDIA Volta GPU.

He holds a Ph.D. in electrical engineering from the Georgia Institute of Technology.

1.5 Really Reaching Human Parity? –Addressing NLP Benchmark Issues on Robustness, Constraint, Bias and Evaluation Metrics

Nan Duan (Microsoft Research Asia)
Qi Zhang (Fudan University)
Ming Zhou (Sinovation Ventures)

We use Machine Reading Comprehension as an example to recap the current status of NLP benchmarks and highlight four key issues with the existing benchmarks including (1) lack of robustness testing on the new independent (but similar) dataset or adversarial inputs, (2) strong constraints on experimental conditions, (3) bias brought by data sampling or human annotation, and (4) lack of suitable evaluation metrics. Then we present our thoughts and experiments on the possible solutions to these challenges from various aspects.

1.6 Machine Understanding in Context

Dave Ferrucci
Founder & CEO, Elemental Cognition
`https://ec.ai/`
davef@ec.ai

The ability for machines to read, understand and reason about natural language would dramatically transform the knowledge economy across all industries. Today's latest Deep Learning marvels do not understand what they read to the extent required for rational problem solving and transparent decision making. And yet we need machines to read, understand and engage with us at a rational level for us to take responsibility for their predictions.

A potential problem slowing the advancement of natural language understanding may be that we are not ambitiously or rigorously defining what it means to comprehend language in the first place. Current metrics and tests may be insufficient to drive the right results. In this talk, I will present a definition of comprehension and early experimental results that strongly suggest existing systems are not up to the task. I will also demonstrate a system architecture and behavior that reflects the sort of language understanding capabilities we envision would do better to advance the field of NLU.

1.6.1 Bio

Dave Ferrucci is an award-winning Artificial Intelligence researcher who started and led the IBM Watson team from its inception through its landmark Jeopardy success in 2011. Dr. Ferrucci's more than 25 years in AI and his passion to see computers fluently think, learn, and communicate inspired him to found Elemental Cognition in 2015. Elemental Cognition is an AI company focused on deep natural language understanding. It explores methods of learning that result in explicable models of intelligence and cross-industry applications.

Dr. Ferrucci graduated from Rensselaer Polytechnic Institute with a Ph.D. in Computer Science. He has over 100 patents and publications. He is an IBM Fellow and has worked at IBM Research and Bridgewater Associates directing their AI research. He has keynoted at highly distinguished venues around the world. Dr. Ferrucci serves as a member of the Connecticut Academy of Science and Engineering and an Adjunct Professor of Entrepreneurship and Innovation at the Kellogg School of Management at Northwestern University.

1.7 Rethinking Benchmarking in AI

Douwe Kiela
Facebook AI Research
`https://douwekiela.github.io/`
@douwekiela on Twitter

The current benchmarking paradigm in AI has many issues: benchmarks saturate quickly, are susceptible to overfitting, contain exploitable annotator artifacts, have unclear or imperfect evaluation metrics, and do not necessarily measure what we really care about. I will talk about our work in trying to rethink the way we do benchmarking in AI, specifically in natural language processing, focusing mostly on the Dynabench platform.

1.7.1 Bio

Douwe Kiela is a Research Scientist at Facebook AI Research, working on natural language processing and multimodal reasoning and understanding. His work has mainly been focused on representation learning, grounded language learning and multi-agent communication. Recently, he has become interested in improving the way we evaluate AI systems.

1.8 The Dawn of Benchmarking

John Makhoul

Benchmarking, or common evaluations, can be traced back to a speech recognition workshop in 1987 that pitted a knowledge- or rule-based method against an automatically trainable method on an evaluation task with a defined corpus. The workshop was part of the DARPA Strategic Computing Program. Deciding on an evaluation metric was a contentious issue that was settled soon after into the currently used word error rate. Program managers at DARPA continued to champion the idea of metrics-based common evaluations with defined training and test corpora and, by inviting international research groups to participate in these annual common evaluations, this benchmarking paradigm took hold and spread to other DARPA programs and internationally. DARPA also provided seed funding for the establishment of the Linguistic Data Consortium, which was instrumental in making common corpora available to the world at large.

1.8.1 Bio

John Makhoul is a Chief Scientist at Raytheon BBN Technologies, Cambridge, MA, where he has been working on various aspects of speech and language processing, including speech analysis and synthesis, speech coding, speech recognition, speech enhancement, artificial neural networks, human-machine interaction using voice, optical character recognition, machine translation, and cross-lingual information retrieval. He is a Fellow of the IEEE, the International Speech Communication Association (ISCA), and the Acoustical Society of America. Makhoul is the recipient of the ISCA medal and several IEEE awards, including the Flanagan medal in speech and audio processing.

1.9 Benchmarking as a Method for Long-Term Research Management: The Common Task Method

Mark Liberman
Linguistic Data Consortium, University of Pennsylvania

Over the course of half a century, DARPA's Human Language Technology program created capabilities such as speech recognition, machine translation, and text understanding, turning them from science fiction fantasies to everyday practical fact. This sustained success was based on the development of the Common Task Method, which allowed decades of incremental progress in advance of commercial viability. I'll describe the origin and (sometimes counter-intuitive) progress of this method, distinguish it from other uses of benchmarking, and speculate about its future.

1.9.1 Bio

Mark Liberman is the Christopher H. Browne Professor of Linguistics at the University of Pennsylvania, with positions in the department of computer science and in the psychology graduate group. He is also founder and director of the Linguistic Data Consortium. Before coming to the University of Pennsylvania, he was head of the linguistics research department at AT&T Bell Laboratories.

1.10 Detection of Dementia from Speech Samples

Brian MacWhinney (Language Technologies and Modern Languages, CMU)
Saturnino Luz (University of Edinburgh)
`https://www.research.ed.ac.uk/en/persons/saturnino-luz-filho`

Diagnosis or early detection of the onset of dementia is important for interventions and planning for life-style changes. Ideally, we would like to achieve accurate diagnosis based on samples of naturalistic language production, as well as samples ellicited using some standard formats, such as narrative, script reading, or picture description. Currently, research in this area relies primarily on the Pitt Corpus in DementiaBank which includes cookie theft narratives from 104 controls, 208 persons with dementia, and 85 persons with unknown diagnosis. These data were used in the ADReSS challenge for INTERSPEECH2020 and will be used in a new challenge for 2021. The previous challenge used hand-created transcripts. The new challenge focuses on a pipeline that can be applied automatically, using ASR and NLP methods. The four major gaps in the current data set are: 1) we need fuller ancillariy data on cognitive and medical status, 2) we need longitudinal data on progression, 3) we need more data across language task and interaction types, and 4) ideally, we would like to have data recorded in the home with voice assistant technology. Currently, challenge participants are committed to open sharing of algorithms, but we need more sharing of primary language data, including data outside of English.

1.10.1 Bios

Brian MacWhinney is Teresa Heinz Professor of Psychology, Computational Linguistics, and Modern Languages at Carnegie Mellon University. His Unified Competition Model analyzes first and second language learning as aspects of a single basic system. He has developed a series of 13 TalkBank open access online databases for the study of language learning, multilingualism, and language disorders. The databases for language disorders include AphasiaBank, ASDBank, DementiaBank, FluencyBank, RHDBank, and TBIBank. These databases provide transcriptions of spoken language linked to audio and video media, along with programs for analysis and linguistic profiling. His other research topics include methods for online learning of second language vocabulary and grammar, neural network modeling of lexical development, fMRI studies of children with focal brain lesions, ERP studies of between-language competition, and the role of embodied perspectival imagery in sentence processing.

Dr. Luz is a reader in medical informatics at the Usher Institute, Edinburgh medical School. His is interested in the use of computational methods in the study of behavioural changes caused by neurodegenerative diseases, with focus on vocalisation and linguistic behaviour. He has also studied interaction in multidisciplinary medical team meetings, doctor-patient consultations, telemedicine and patient safety.

1.11 Lessons from SPEC

John Mashey
https://en.wikipedia.org/wiki/John_Mashey
https://www.spec.org/benchmarks.html
Twitter: @johnmashey
(Mashey, 2004, 2005)
https://bits.blogs.nytimes.com/2013/02/01/the-origins-of-big-data-an-etymological-detective-story

In the 1980s, amidst fierce competition among new microprocessor architectures, CPU benchmarking was in poor condition. Many commonly-used benchmarks were small synthetic benchmarks like Whetstone and Dhrystone that poorly-matched realistic programs. Companies sometimes outright cheated by special-casing compilers to recognize major benchmarks. Some vendors honestly reported results from realistic benchmarks, but even when running the same programs, often used different inputs, so that potential customers could not easily make direct comparisons. Many customers did not trust performance claims.

The talk reviews the odd way SPEC got started in 1988, initially by MIPS, Apollo, Hewlett-Packard and Sun, later joined by many others, then covers the ground rules that evolved to let fierce competitors work together successfully to produce benchmarks that became industry standards and exemplars of good methodologies for selecting benchmarks, validating results, reporting them carefully and deciding when they had to be retired as obsolete for one reason or another.

SPEC of course is still active, 30+ years later. The talk reviews lessons learned about high-stakes benchmarking, evolution of benchmark suites over time, competitor social issues, credibility issues when people think the foxes are guarding the hen-house, as we were asked by a member of the press. From the beginning, SPEC reported performance on a set of benchmarks as a set of ratios versus a base system, so that people could find benchmarks they thought relevant to their own and ignore the others. Many arguments had occurred over summary means, but as had been done in some performance reports, SPEC correctly used the Geometric Mean, but without really delving into the underlying statistics, which only happened in 2004.

A set of benchmark ratios can be viewed as a sample (representative if selected by experts) from a large population of programs. In practice, many sets of benchmark ratios are well-fit by the log-normal distribution, whose mean is the Geometric Mean, but also allows computation of a (Multiplicative) Standard Deviation, Confidence Intervals, etc. The talk briefly reviews the relevant, simple statistics and the rationale for them.

1.11.1 Bio

John Mashey is a semi-retired computer scientist/corporate executive at Bell Labs, Convergent Technologies, MIPS Computer Systems and Silicon Graphics, where he is was originator of the phrase "Big Data" (according to NY Times). He later consulted for venture capitalists, advised startups and occasionally consulted for companies like Nvidia. He is a 20-year Trustee at the Computer History Museum. He was one of the 4 cofounders of the SPEC benchmarking group in 1988 and was asked in 2018 to advise the MLperf benchmarking group on relevant statistics.

1.12 Benchmarking for diarization. Lessons from the DIHARD evaluation series

Neville Ryant
Linguistic Data Consortium, University of Pennsylvania

Recently, there has been renewed interest in speaker diarization – that is, the task of determining "who spoke when" in a recording. With this renewed interest has come major improvements in system performance with error rates for the DIHARD challenge falling by 33in the span of 4 years. However, despite these successes, the goal of truly robust diarization which is resilient to the full range of natural variation in recordings (e.g., conversational domain, recording equipment, reverberation, ambient noise) remains elusive. In this talk we will review the evolution of the state-of-the-art on multiple domains from the DIHARD dataset as well as some challenges we have encountered in attempting to construct a representative diarization benchmark.

1.12.1 Bio

Neville Ryant is a researcher at the Linguistic Data Consortium (LDC) at the University of Pennsylvania, where he has worked on many topics in speech recognition including: forced alignment, speech activity detection, large scale corpus linguistics, computational paralinguistics, and automated analysis of tone. Since 2017, he has been the principal organizer of the DIHARD challenge, the most recent iteration of which (DIHARD III) completed in December 2020.

1.13 5 Ways to Make Your Data More Relevant

Anders Søgaard
University of Copenhagen
`https://anderssoegaard.github.io/`

This talk briefly summarizes works I've been involved in that propose improvements to how we evaluate our models, e.g., presenting sampling strategies that better simulate real-life scenarios. The talk will be a sort of self help talk with simple, practical advice for how to add value to your existing data.

1.14 Benchmarking and TREC

Ellen Voorhees
National Institute of Standards and Technology

urlhttps://www.nist.gov/people/ellen-m-voorhees

Coopetitions are activities in which competitors cooperate for a common good. Community evaluations such as the Text REtrieval Conference (TREC) are prototypical examples of coopetitions in information retrieval (IR) and have now been a part of the field for thirty years. This longevity and the proliferation of shared evaluation tasks suggest that, indeed, the net impact of community evaluations is positive. But what are these benefits, and what are the attendant costs?

This talk will use TREC tracks as case studies to explore the benefits and disadvantages of different evaluation task designs. Coopetitions can improve state-of-the-art effectiveness for a retrieval task by establishing a research cohort and constructing the infrastructure—including problem definition, test collections, scoring metrics, and research methodology—necessary to make progress on the task. They can also facilitate technology transfer and amortize the infrastructure costs. The primary danger of coopetitions is for an entire research community to overfit to some peculiarity of the evaluation task. This risk can be minimized by building multiple test sets and regularly updating the evaluation task.]

1.14.1 Bio

Ellen Voorhees is a Senior Research Scientist at the US National Institute of Standards and Technology (NIST). Her primary responsibility at NIST is to manage the Text REtrieval Conference (TREC) project, a project that develops the infrastructure required for large-scale evaluation of search engines and other information access technology. Voorhees' research focuses on developing and validating appropriate evaluation schemes to measure system effectiveness for diverse user tasks.

Voorhees is a fellow of the ACM and an inaugural member of the ACM SIGIR Academy. She has published numerous articles on information retrieval techniques and evaluation methodologies and serves on the review boards of several journals and conferences.

1.15 Benchmarks: An Industry Perspective

Hua Wu and **Jing Liu**
Baidu
https://wuhuanlp.github.io/
https://www.machinereading.ai/

In recent years, the researchers from academia created large-scale datasets mainly in a crowdsourcing way, that accelerate the development of NLP technology. However, these datasets might present different distributions and different challenges from the ones in real-world applications. In this talk, we will introduce our efforts on building NLP benchmarks from an industry perspective. Specifically, we will describe our released datasets on the tasks including question answering, dialogue and simultaneous translation that were created to tackle with the problems in industrial applications. We will present the challenges of these datasets and show how these datasets drive the advancements of NLP technologies. Additionally, we will talk about LUGE, which is an Open-Source Project of Chinese NLP benchmarks. LUGE aims to evaluate NLP models in terms of robustness and adaptability across multiple tasks and multiple domains, which are very crucial for their success in industrial applications.

1.15.1 Bios

Hua Wu is the chair of Baidu tech committee and tech leader of Baidu NLP. Before that, she worked for Toshiba (China) R&D center and Microsoft Research Asia. She obtained her Ph.D. degree from Institute of Automation, Chinese Academy of Science in 2001. Her research interests span a wide range of topics including machine translation, dialogue systems, knowledge graph, etc. She was the Program Co-Chair of ACL 2014 and AACL 2020 (Asia-Pacific Chapter of ACL).

Jing Liu is a principal architect and a tech leader of deep question answering team at Baidu NLP since 2017. Before that, he was a researcher at Microsoft Research Asia (MSRA). He obtained Ph.D. degree in computer science from Harbin Institute of Technology (HIT) in 2014. He is interested broadly in natural language processing and information retrieval, with a particular focus on building robust end-to-end question answering system. He published over 30 research papers in prestigious conferences including ACL, EMNLP, NAACL, SIGIR, WSDM, CIKM, etc. He served as an Area Chair in ACL 2021.

References

Jesse Dunietz, Gregory Burnham, Akash Bharadwaj, Owen Rambow, Jennifer Chu-Carroll, and David Ferrucci. 2020. To test machine comprehension, start by defining comprehension. *arXiv preprint arXiv:2005.01525*.

John R Mashey. 2004. War of the benchmark means: time for a truce. *ACM SIGARCH Computer Architecture News*, 32(4):1–14.

John R Mashey. 2005. Summarizing performance is no mean feat [computer performance analysis]. In *IEEE International. 2005 Proceedings of the IEEE Workload Characterization Symposium, 2005.*, pages 1–1. IEEE Computer Society.

Guideline Bias in Wizard-of-Oz Dialogues

Victor Petrén Bach Hansen,[1 2] **Anders Søgaard**[1]
[1]Department of Computer Science, University of Copenhagen, Denmark
[2]Topdanmark A/S, Denmark
{victor.petren, soegaard}@di.ku.dk

Abstract

NLP models struggle with generalization due to sampling and annotator bias. This paper focuses on a different kind of bias that has received very little attention: *guideline bias*, i.e., the bias introduced by how our annotator guidelines are formulated. We examine two recently introduced dialogue datasets, CCPE-M and Taskmaster-1, both collected by trained assistants in a Wizard-of-Oz set-up. For CCPE-M, we show how a simple lexical bias for the word *like* in the guidelines biases the data collection. This bias, in effect, leads to poor performance on data without this bias: a preference elicitation architecture based on BERT suffers a 5.3% absolute drop in performance, when *like* is replaced with a synonymous phrase, and a 13.2% drop in performance when evaluated on out-of-sample data. For Taskmaster-1, we show how the order in which instructions are presented, biases the data collection.

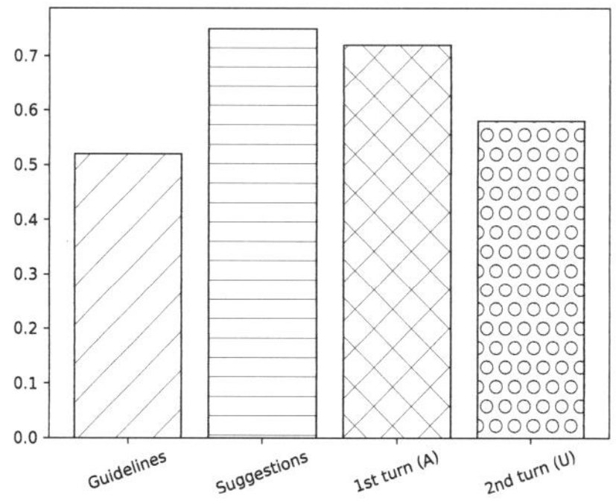

Figure 1: The percentage of sentences with the word *like* in the CCPE-M annotation guidelines (Guidelines), the suggested questions to ask users, in the guidelines (Suggestions), (c) the *actual* first turns by the assistants (1st turn), and (d) the actual replies by the users (2nd turn). In all cases, more than half of the sentences contain the word *like*.

1 Introduction

Sample bias is a well-known problem in NLP – discussed from Marcus (1982) to Barrett et al. (2019) – and annotator bias has been discussed as far back as Ratnaparkhi (1996). This paper focuses on a different kind of bias that has received very little attention: *guideline bias*, i.e., the bias introduced by how our annotator guidelines are formulated.

Annotation guidelines are used to train annotators, and guidelines are therefore in some sense intended to and designed to prime annotators. What we will refer to in our discussion of guideline bias, is rather the unintended biases that result from how guidelines are formulated, and the examples used in those guidelines. If a treebank annotation guideline focuses overly on parasitic gap constructions, for example, inter-annotator agreement may be higher on those, and annotators may be biased to annotate similar phenomena by analogy with parasitic gaps.

We focus on two recently introduced datasets, the Coached Conversational Preference Elicitation corpus (CCPE-M) from Radlinski et al. (2019), related to the task of conversational recommendation (Christakopoulou et al., 2016; Li et al., 2018), and Taskmaster-1 (Byrne et al., 2019), which is a multi-purpose, multi-domain dialogue dataset. CCPE-M consists of conversations about movie preferences, and the part of Taskmaster-1, we focus on here, conversations about theatre ticket reservations. Both corpora were collected by having a team of assistants interact with users in a Wizard-of-Oz (WoZ) set-up, i.e. a human plays the role of a digital assistant which engages a user in a conversation about their movie preferences. The assistants were given a set of guidelines in advance, as part of their training, and it is these guidelines that induce biases. In CCPE-M, it is the overwhelming use of the verb *like* (see Figure 5) and its trickle-down effects, we focus on; in Taskmaster-1, the order of

Proceedings of the 1st Workshop on Benchmarking: Past, Present and Future, pages 8–14
August 5–6, 2021. ©2021 Association for Computational Linguistics

the instructions. In fact, the CCPE-M guidelines consist of 324 words, of which 20 (**6%**) are inflections or derivations of the lemma *like*: As shown in Figure 5 in the Appendix, more than **50%** of the sentences in the guidelines include forms of *like*! This very strong bias in the guidelines has a clear downstream effect on the assistants that are collecting the data. In their first dialogue turn, the assistants use the word *like* in **72%** of the dialogues. This again biases the users responding to the assistants in the WoZ set-up: In **58%** of their first turns, given that the assistant uses a form of the word *like*, they also use the verb *like*. We show that this bias leads to overly optimistic estimates of performance. Additionally, we also demonstrate how the guideline affects the user responses through a controlled priming experiment. For Taskmaster-1, we show a similar effect of the guidelines on the collected dialogues.

Contributions We introduce the notion of *guideline bias* and present a detailed analysis of guideline bias in two recently introduced dialogue corpora (CCPE-M and Taskmaster-1). Our main experiments focus on CCPE-M: We show how a simple bias toward the verb *like* easily leads us to overestimate performance in the wild by showing performance drops on semantically innocent perturbations of the test data, as well as on a new sample of movie preference elicitations that we collected from Reddit for the purpose of this paper. We also show that debiasing the data, improves performance. The CCPE-M provides a very clear example of *guideline bias*, but other examples can be found, e.g., in Taskmaster-1, which we discuss in §3. We discuss more examples in §4.

2 Bias in CCPE-M

We first examine the CCPE-M dataset of spoken dialogues about movie preferences. The dialogues in CCPE-M are generated in a Wizard-of-Oz set-up, where the assistants type their input, which is then translated into speech using text-to-speech technologies, at which point users respond by speech. The dialogues were transcribed and annotated by the authors of Radlinski et al. (2019).

Sentence classification We frame the CCPE-M movie preference detection problem as a sentence-level classification task. If a sentence contains a labeled span, we let this label percolate to the sentence level and be a label of the entire sentence. If a sentence contains multiple unique label spans the sentence is assigned the leftmost label. A sentence-level label should therefore be interpreted as saying *in this sentence, the user elicits a movie or genre preference*. Our resulting sentence classification dataset contains five different preference labels, including a *NONE* label. We shuffle the data at the dialogue-level and divide the dialogues into training/development/test splits using a 80/10/10 ratio, ensuring sentences from the same dialogue will not end up in both training and test data. As the assistants utterances rarely express any preferences, we only include the user utterances to balance the number of negative labels. See Table 2 for statistics regarding the label distribution.

Original

I [*like*] Terminator 2

Perturbed

I [*love*] Terminator 2

I [*was incredibly affected by*] Terminator 2

I [*have as my all time favorite movie*] Terminator 2

I [*am out of this world passionate about*] Terminator 2

Figure 2: Example of test sentence permutations.

Perturbations of test data In order to analyse the effects of guideline bias in the CCPE-M dataset, we introduce perturbations of the instances in the test set where *like* occurs, replacing *like* with a synonymous word, e.g. *love*, or paraphrase, e.g. *holds dearly*. We experiment with four different replacements for *like*: (i) *love*, (ii) *was incredibly affected by*, (iii) *have as my all time favorite movie* and (iv) *am out of this world passionate about*. See Figure 2 for an example sentence and its perturbed variants. The perturbations occasionally, but rarely, lead to grammatically incorrect input.[1] We emphasize that even though we increase the length of the sentence, the phrases we replace *like* with should signal an even stronger statement of preference, which models should be able to pick up on. Since our data consists of informal speech it includes adverbial uses of *like*; we only replace verb occurrences, relying on SpaCy's POS tagger.[2] We replace 219 instances of the verb *like* throughout the test set.

Perturbations of train data We also augment the training data to create a less biased resource.

[1]Our models are generally robust to such variation, and, as we will see in our experiments below, the perturbations are less harmful than collecting a new sample of evaluation data and evaluating your model on this sample.

[2]`https://spacy.io/`

Testing on (↓)/Training on (→)	CCPE-M		CCPE-M$_{thesaurus}$	
	BiLSTM	BERT	BiLSTM	BERT
CCPE-M	74.79	**79.07**	75.16	78.73
CCPE-M$_{love}$	74.39	78.82	75.43	**78.87**
CCPE-M$_{was\ incredibly\ affected\ by}$	70.32	75.03	73.36	**77.42**
CCPE-M$_{have\ as\ my\ all\ time\ favorite\ movie}$	70.75	74.37	67.85	**76.93**
CCPE-M$_{am\ out\ of\ this\ world\ passionate\ about}$	70.70	73.76	72.84	**78.24**
Reddit	44.55	65.86	46.48	**67.45**

Table 1: Comparison of in-sample F_1 performance, performance on the same data with *like* replaced with phrases with similar meaning, and performance on Reddit data. Results are reported for training models on biased CCPE-M as well as a debiased CCPE-M$_{thesaurus}$ which improves model performance in almost all cases.

Label	train	dev	test	Reddit
NONE	4508	535	545	60
MOVIE_OR_SERIES	2736	346	313	119
MOVIE_GENRE_OR_CATEGORY	1274	169	166	20
PERSON	66	6	9	11
SOMETHING_ELSE	21	0	0	1
total	8605	1056	1033	211

Table 2: CCPE-M and Reddit sentence-level statistics

Here we adopt a slightly different strategy, also to evaluate a model trained on the debiased training data to the above perturbed test data: We use six paraphrases of the verb *like* listed in a publicly available thesaurus,[3] none of which overlap with the words used to perturb the test data, and randomly replace verbal *like* with a probability of 20%. The paraphrases are sampled from a uniform distribution. A total of 401 instances are replaced in the training data using this approach. This is not intended as a solution to guideline bias, but in our experiments below, we show that a model trained on this simple, debiased dataset generalizes better to out of sample data, showing that the bias toward *like* was in fact one of the reasons that our baseline classifier performed poorly in this domain.

Reddit movie preference dataset In addition to the perturbed CCPE-M dataset, we also collect and annotate a challenge dataset from Reddit threads discussing movies for the purpose of preference elicitation. The comments are scraped from Reddit threads with titles such as '*Here's A Simple Question. What's Your Favorite Movie Genre And Why?*' or '*What's a movie that you love that everyone else hates?*' and mostly consist of top-level comments. These top-level comments typically respond directly the question posed by the thread, and explicitly state preferences. We also include some random samples from discussion trees that contain no preferences, to balance the label distribution slightly. In this data, we observe the word *like*, but less frequently: The verb *like* occurred in 15/211 examples. The data is annotated at the sentence level, as described previously, and we follow the methodology described by Radlinski et al. (2019) and identify anchor items such as names of movies or series, genres or categories and then label each sentence according to the preference statements describing said item, if any. The dataset contains roughly 100 comments, that when divided into individual sentences resulting in 211 datapoints. The statistics can be found in the final column of Table 2. We make the data publicly available.[4]

Results We evaluate the performance on two different models on the original and perturbed CCPE-M, as well as on our Reddit data: (i) a bidirectional LSTM (Hochreiter and Schmidhuber, 1997) sentence classifier, trained only on CCPE-M, including the embeddings, and (ii) a fine-tuned BERT sentence classification model (Devlin et al., 2018). For (i), we use two BiLSTM layers ($d = 128$), randomly initialized embeddings ($d = 64$), and a dropout rate of 0.5. The model is trained for 45 epochs. For (ii), we use the base, uncased BERT model with the default parameters and finetune for 3 epochs. Model selection is conducted based on performance on the development set. Performance is measured using class-weighted F_1 score. We report results in Table 1 on the various perturbation test sets as well as the Reddit data, when (i) the models are trained on the unchanged CCPE-M data, and (ii) the models are trained on the debiased version CCPE-M$_{thesaurus}$.

[3] `http://thesaurus.com`. The paraphrases consists of: (1) *derive pleasure from*, (2) *get a kick out of*, (3) *appreciate*, (4) *take an interest in*, (5) *cherish*, (6) *find appealing*.

[4] `https://github.com/vpetren/guideline_bias`

On the original dataset, BERT performs slightly better than the BiLSTM architecture, but the differences are relatively small. Both BiLSTM and BERT suffer a drop in performance, when examples are perturbed and the word *like* is replaced with synonymous words or phrases. Note how longer substitutions result in a larger drop in performance, e.g. *love* vs. *am out of this world passionate about*. We see the drops follow the same pattern for both architectures, while BiLSTM seems a bit more sensitive to our test permutations. Both models do even worse on our newly collected Reddit data. Here, we clearly see the sensitivity of the BiLSTM architecture, which suffers a 30% absolute drop in F_1; but even BERT suffers a bit performance drop of more than 13%, when evaluated on a new sample of data. When training on CCPE-$M_{thesaurus}$, both models become more invariant to our perturbations,with up to 4.5 F_1 improvements for BERT model and 3 F_1 improvements for the BiLSTM, without any loss of performance on the original test set. We also observe improvements on our collected Reddit data, suggesting that *the initial drop in performance can be partially explained by guideline bias and not only domain differences.*

Controlled priming experiment To establish the priming effect of guidelines in a more controlled setting, we set up a small crowdsourced experiment. We asked turkers to respond to a hypothetical question about movie preferences. For example, turkers were asked to imagine they are in a situation in which they 'are asked what movies' they 'like', and that they like a specific movie, say *Harry Potter*. The turker may then respond: *I've always liked Harry Potter*. We collected 40 user responses for each of the priming verbs *like*, *love* and *prefer*, 120 total, and for each of the verbs used to prime the turkers, we compute a probability distribution over most of the verbs in the response vocabulary that are likely to be used to describe a general preference towards something. Figure 3 shows the results of the crowdsourced priming experiments. We can observe that when a specific priming word, such as *like*, is used, there is a significantly higher probability that the response from the user will contain that same word, illustrating that when keywords in guidelines are heavily overrepresented, the collected data will also reflect this bias.

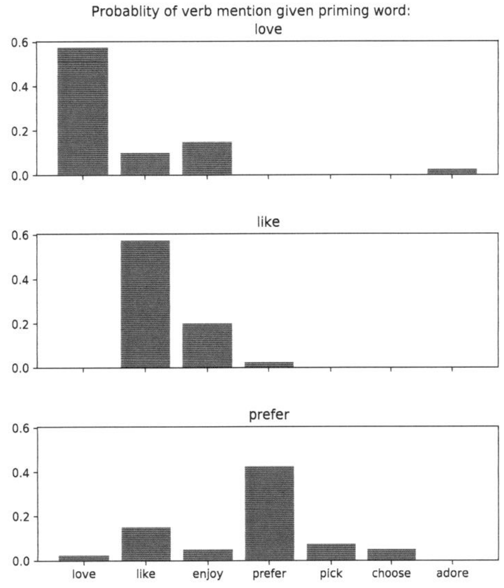

Figure 3: Probability that a verb that describes a preference towards a movie is mentioned, given a priming word by the annotator is mentioned.

3 Bias in Taskmaster-1

The order in which the goals of the conversation is described to annotators in the guidelines can also bias the order in which these goals are pursued in conversation. Taskmaster-1 contains conversations between a user and an agent where the user seeks to accomplish a *goal* by, e.g., booking tickets to a movie, which is the domain we focus on. When booking tickets to go see a movie, we can specify the movie title before the theatre, or vice versa, but models may not become robust to such variation if exposed to very biased examples.

Unlike CCPE-M, the Taskmaster-1 dataset was (wisely) collected using two different sets of guidelines to reduce bias, and we can therefore investigate the downstream effects of of the bias induced by the two sets of guidelines. To quantify the guideline bias, we compute the probability that a goal x_1 is mentioned before another one x_2 in an dialogue, given that x_1 precedes x_2 in the guidelines. We only consider dialogues where all goals are mentioned at least once, i.e., $\sim$ 900 in total; the conversations are then divided into two, based on the guideline that was used. Figure 4 shows the heat map of these relative probabilities. The guidelines have a clear influence on the final structure of the conversation, i.e. if the movie title (x_1) is mentioned before the city (x_2) in the guideline, there is

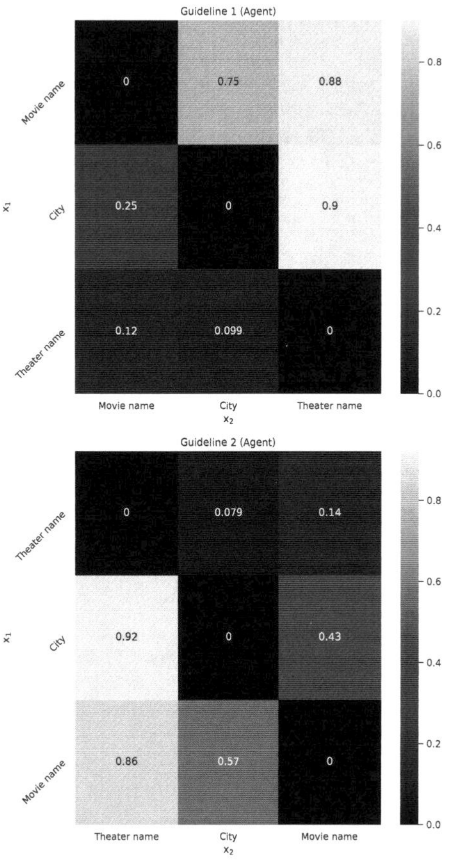

Figure 4: Probability that a guideline goal x_1 is mentioned before another one x_2 in an actual dialogue, given that x_1 comes before x_2 in the agent's guideline.

a high probability (0.75) that the same is true in the dialogues. If they are not, the probability is much lower (0.57).

4 Related Work

Plank et al. (2014) present an approach to correcting for adjudicator biases. Bender and Friedman (2018) raise the possibility of (demographic) bias in annotation guidelines, but do not provide a means for detecting such biases or show any existing datasets to be biased in this way. Amidei et al. (2018) also discuss the possibility, but in a footnote. Geva et al. (2019) investigates how crowdsourcing practices can introduce annotator biases in NLU datasets and therefore result in models overestimating confidence on samples from annotators that have contributed to both the training and test sets. Liu et al. (2018), on the other hand, discuss a case in which annotation guidelines are biased by being developed for a particular domain and not easily applicable to another. Cohn and Specia (2013) explores how models can learn from annotator bias in a somewhat opposite scenario from ours, e.g. when annotators deviate from annotation guidelines and inject their own bias into the data, and by using multi-task learning to train annotator specific models, they improve performance by leveraging annotation (dis)agreements. There are, to the best of our knowledge, relatively few examples of researchers identifying concrete guideline-related bias in benchmark datasets: Dickinson (2003) suggest that POS annotation in the English Penn Treebank is biased by the vagueness of the annotation guidelines in some respects. Friedrich et al. (2015) report a similar guideline-induced bias in the ACE datasets. Dandapat et al. (2009) discuss an interesting bias in a Bangla/Hindi POS-annotated corpus arising from a decision in the annotation guidelines to include two labels for when annotators were uncertain, but not specifying in detail how these labels were to be used. Goldberg and Elhadad (2010) define structural bias for dependency parsing and how it can be attributed to bias in individual datasets, among other factors, originating from their annotation schemes. Ibanez and Ohtani (2014) report a similar case, where ambiguity in how special categories were defined, led to bias in a corpus of Spanish learner errors.

5 Discussion & Conclusion

In this work, we examined *guideline bias* in two newly presented WoZ style dialogue corpora: We showed how a lexical bias for the word *like* in the annotation guidelines of CCPE-M, through a controlled priming experiment leads to a bias for this word in the dialogues, and that models trained on this corpus are sensitive to the absence of this verb. We provided a new test dataset for this task, collected from Reddit, and show how a debiased model performs better on this dataset, suggesting the 13% drop is in part the result of guideline bias. We showed a similar bias in Taskmaster-1.

Acknowledgements

This work was funded by the Innovation Fund Denmark and Topdanmark.

References

Jacopo Amidei, Paul Piwek, and Alistair Willis. 2018. Rethinking the agreement in human evaluation tasks. In *COLING*.

Maria Barrett, Yova Kementchedjhieva, Yanai Elazar, Desmond Elliott, and Anders Søgaard. 2019. Adversarial removal of demographic attributes revisited. In *EMNLP*.

Emily Bender and Batya Friedman. 2018. Data statements for natural language processing: Toward mitigating system bias and enabling better science. In *TACL*.

Bill Byrne, Karthik Krishnamoorthi, Chinnadhurai Sankar, Arvind Neelakantan, Ben Goodrich, Daniel Duckworth, Semih Yavuz, Amit Dubey, Kyu-Young Kim, and Andy Cedilnik. 2019. Taskmaster-1: Toward a realistic and diverse dialog dataset. In *Proceedings of the 2019 Conference on Empirical Methods in Natural Language Processing and the 9th International Joint Conference on Natural Language Processing (EMNLP-IJCNLP)*, pages 4516–4525, Hong Kong, China. Association for Computational Linguistics.

Konstantina Christakopoulou, Filip Radlinski, and Katja Hofmann. 2016. Towards conversational recommender systems. In *Proceedings of the 22Nd ACM SIGKDD International Conference on Knowledge Discovery and Data Mining*, KDD '16, pages 815–824, New York, NY, USA. ACM.

Trevor Cohn and Lucia Specia. 2013. Modelling annotator bias with multi-task Gaussian processes: An application to machine translation quality estimation. In *Proceedings of the 51st Annual Meeting of the Association for Computational Linguistics (Volume 1: Long Papers)*, pages 32–42, Sofia, Bulgaria. Association for Computational Linguistics.

Sandipan Dandapat, Priyanka Biswas, Monojit Choudhury, and Kalika Bali. 2009. Complex linguistic annotation – no easy way out! a case from bangla and hindi pos labeling tasks. In *LAW*.

Jacob Devlin, Ming-Wei Chang, Kenton Lee, and Kristina Toutanova. 2018. BERT: pre-training of deep bidirectional transformers for language understanding. *CoRR*, abs/1810.04805.

Markus Dickinson. 2003. Detecting errors in part-of-speech annotation. In *EACL*.

Annemarie Friedrich, Alexis Palmer, Melissa Peate Sørensen, and Manfred Pinkal. 2015. Annotating genericity: a survey, a scheme, and a corpus. In *LAW*.

Mor Geva, Yoav Goldberg, and Jonathan Berant. 2019. Are we modeling the task or the annotator? an investigation of annotator bias in natural language understanding datasets. In *Proceedings of the 2019 Conference on Empirical Methods in Natural Language Processing and the 9th International Joint Conference on Natural Language Processing (EMNLP-IJCNLP)*, pages 1161–1166, Hong Kong, China. Association for Computational Linguistics.

Yoav Goldberg and Michael Elhadad. 2010. Inspecting the structural biases of dependency parsing algorithms. In *Proceedings of the Fourteenth Conference on Computational Natural Language Learning*, pages 234–242, Uppsala, Sweden. Association for Computational Linguistics.

Sepp Hochreiter and Jürgen Schmidhuber. 1997. Long short-term memory. *Neural Comput.*, 9(8):1735–1780.

Maria Del Pilar Valverde Ibanez and Akira Ohtani. 2014. Annotating article errors in spanish learner texts: design and evaluation of an annotation scheme. In *PACLIC*.

Raymond Li, Samira Ebrahimi Kahou, Hannes Schulz, Vincent Michalski, Laurent Charlin, and Chris Pal. 2018. Towards deep conversational recommendations. In S. Bengio, H. Wallach, H. Larochelle, K. Grauman, N. Cesa-Bianchi, and R. Garnett, editors, *Advances in Neural Information Processing Systems 31*, pages 9725–9735. Curran Associates, Inc.

Yijia Liu, Yi Zhu, Wanxiang Che, Bing Qin, Nathan Schneider, and Noah Smith. 2018. Parsing tweets into universal dependencies. In *NAACL*.

Mitch Marcus. 1982. Building non-normative systems – the search for robustness. In *ACL*.

Barbara Plank, Dirk Hovy, and Anders Søgaard. 2014. Learning part-of-speech taggers with inter-annotator agreement loss. In *EACL*.

Filip Radlinski, Krisztian Balog, Bill Byrne, and Karthik Krishnamoorthi. 2019. Coached conversational preference elicitation: A case study in understanding movie preferences. In *SigDial*.

Adwait Ratnaparkhi. 1996. A maximum entropy model for part-of-speech tagging. In *EMNLP*.

A Appendices

General Instructions The goal of this type of dialogue is for you to get the users to explain their movie preferences: The KIND of movies they like and dislike and WHY. We really want to end up finding out WHY they like what they like movie AND why the DON'T like what they don't like. We want them to take lots of turns to explain these things to you.

Important We want users to discuss likes and dislikes for kinds of movies rather than just about specific movies. (But we trigger these more general preferences based on remembering certain titles.) You may bring up particular movie titles in order to get them thinking about why they like or dislike that kind of thing. Do not bring up particular directors, actors, or genres. For each session do the following steps:

1. Start with a normal introduction: Hello. I'd like to discuss your movie preferences.

2. Ask them what kind of movies they like and why they generally like that kind of movie.

3. Ask them for a particular movie name they liked.

4. Ask them what about that KIND of movie they liked. (get a couple of reasons at least – let them go on if they choose)

5. Ask them to name a particular movie they did not like.

6. Ask them what about that movie they did not like. (get a couple of reasons at least or let them go on if they choose)

7. Now choose a movies using the movie generator link below. Ask them if they liked that movie (if they haven't seen it: (a) ask if they have heard of it. If so, ask if they would see it (b) then choose another that they have seen to ask about). Once you find a movie from the list they have seen, ask them why they liked or disliked that kind of movie (get a couple of reasons).

8. Finally, end the conversation gracefully

Figure 5: CCPE-M Guidelines to Assistants

We Need to Consider Disagreement in Evaluation

Valerio Basile[*] ♣, Michael Fell♣, Tommaso Fornaciari♦, Dirk Hovy♦, Silviu Paun♥, Barbara Plank♠, Massimo Poesio♥, Alexandra Uma♥
♣University of Turin, ♦Bocconi University
♥Queen Mary University of London, ♠IT University of Copenhagen
♣{valerio.basile, michaelkurt.fell}@unito.it
♦{dirk.hovy, fornaciari.tommaso}@unibocconi.it
♥{s.paun, m.poesio, a.n.uma}@qmul.ac.uk, ♠bplank@itu.dk

Abstract

Evaluation is of paramount importance in data-driven research fields such as Natural Language Processing (NLP) and Computer Vision (CV). But current evaluation practice in NLP, except for end-to-end tasks such as machine translation, spoken dialogue systems, or NLG, largely hinges on the existence of a single "ground truth" against which we can meaningfully compare the prediction of a model. However, this assumption is flawed for two reasons. 1) In many cases, more than one answer is correct. 2) Even where there is a single answer, disagreement among annotators is ubiquitous, making it difficult to decide on a gold standard. We discuss three sources of disagreement: from the annotator, the data, and the context, and show how this affects even seemingly objective tasks. Current methods of adjudication, agreement, and evaluation ought to be reconsidered at the light of this evidence. Some researchers now propose to address this issue by minimizing disagreement, creating cleaner datasets. We argue that such a simplification is likely to result in oversimplified models just as much as it would do for end-to-end tasks such as machine translation. Instead, we suggest that we need to improve today's evaluation practice to better capture such disagreement. Datasets with multiple annotations are becoming more common, as are methods to integrate disagreement into modeling. The logical next step is to extend this to evaluation.

1 Introduction

Evaluation is of paramount importance to Natural Language Processing (NLP) and Computer Vision (CV). Automatic evaluation is the primary mechanism to drive and measure progress due to its simplicity and efficiency (Resnik and Lin, 2010; Church and Hestness, 2019). However,

Figure 1: What is the ground truth? Examples from VQA v2 (Goyal et al., 2017) and (Gimpel et al., 2011).

today's evaluation practice for virtually all NLP tasks concerned with a fundamental aspect of language interpretation–POS tagging, word sense disambiguation, named entity recognition, coreference, relation extraction, natural language inference, or sentiment analysis– is seriously flawed: the candidate hypotheses of a system (i.e., its predictions) are compared against an evaluation set that is assumed to encode a "ground truth" for the modeling task. Yet this evaluation model is outdated and needs reconsideration. The notion of a single correct answer ignores the subjectivity and complexity of many tasks, and focuses on "easy", low-risk evaluation, holding back progress in the field. We discuss three sources of disagreement: from the annotator, the data, and the context.

The underlying assumption of the current approach is that the evaluation set represents the

[*] Authors in alphabetical order.

Proceedings of the 1st Workshop on Benchmarking: Past, Present and Future, pages 15–21
August 5–6, 2021. ©2021 Association for Computational Linguistics

best possible approximation of the truth about a given phenomenon, or at least a reasonable one. This ground truth is usually obtained by developing an annotation scheme for the task aiming to achieve the highest possible agreement between human annotators (Artstein and Poesio, 2008). Disagreements between annotators are either reconciled by hand or aggregated (particularly in the case of crowdsourced annotations) to extract the most likely or agreed-upon choices (Hovy et al., 2013; Passonneau and Carpenter, 2013; Paun et al., 2018). This aggregated data is referred to as "gold standard" (see Ide and Pustejovsky (2017) for an in-depth analysis of annotation methodology).

However, there is plenty of evidence that gold labels are an idealization, and that unreconcilable disagreement is abundant. Figure 1 shows two examples from CV and NLP. This is particularly true for tasks involving highly subjective judgments, such as hate speech detection (Akhtar et al., 2019, 2020) or sentiment analysis (Kenyon-Dean et al., 2018). However, it is not a trivial issue even in more linguistic tasks, such as part-of-speech tagging (Plank et al., 2014), word sense disambiguation (Passonneau et al., 2012; Jurgens, 2013), or coreference resolution (Poesio and Artstein, 2005; Recasens et al., 2011). Systematic disagreement also exists in image classification tasks, where labels may overlap (Rodrigues and Pereira, 2018; Peterson et al., 2019). Disagreement and task difficulty and subjectivity also challenge traditional agreement measures (Artstein and Poesio, 2008). High agreement is typically used as a proxy for data quality. However, it obscures possible sources of disagreement (Poesio and Artstein, 2005). We summarize some of the evidence on disagreement in Section 2.

The need for metrics not based on the assumption that a gold standard exists has long been accepted for end-to-end tasks, particularly those involving an aspect of natural language generation, such as conversational agents, machine translation, surface realisation, image captioning, or summarization. Metrics such as BLEU for machine translation/generation, ROUGE for summarization, or NDCG for ranking Web searches all support more than one gold standard reference. Shared tasks in this areas (particularly on paraphrasing), have also considered the role of disagreement in their evaluation metrics (Butnariu et al., 2009; Hendrickx et al., 2013). Variability in the annotation is a feature of many such tasks (see, e.g., van der Lee et al. (2019) for agreement issues in generated text evaluation) even though many corpora still may come with single references due to data collection costs. High agreement is disfavored, and even bears risks of non-natural, highly homogenized system outputs for generation tasks (Amidei et al., 2018). The main argument of this position paper is that we should recognize that the same issues, if perhaps in less extreme version, apply to the analysis tasks we discuss here.

In recent years, proposals have been put forward to consider the disagreement as informative content that can be leveraged to improve task performance (Plank et al., 2014; Aroyo and Welty, 2015; Jamison and Gurevych, 2015). Uma et al. (2020) and Basile (2020) investigated the impact of disagreement-informed data on the quality of NLP evaluation, and found it to be beneficial and providing complementary information, as further discussed in Section 3. This led them to organize a first shared task on learning from disagreement and providing non-aggregated benchmarks for evaluation (Uma et al., 2021).

In contrast with this trend, Bowman and Dahl (2021) recently proposed to study biases and artifacts in data to eliminate them. Beigman Klebanov and Beigman (2009) adopt a slightly softer stance, proposing to only evaluating on "easy" (as in, highly agreed upon) instances. Based on the evidence about the prevalence of disagreement in NLP judgments, we argue against this approach. First, it leads to information loss in the attempt to reducing noise in the data. Second, it is unnecessary: while evaluation methods that include disagreement are not yet established, several methodologies already do exist. Removing the disagreement might lead to better evaluation scores, but it fundamentally hides the true nature of the task we are trying to solve.

2 Disagreement in NLP

In this section, we outline three possible sources of disagreement. Afterward, we describe how disagreement has been studied in objective and arguably more subjective tasks in NLP.

2.1 Sources of Disagreement

Annotation implies an interaction between the human judge, the instance which has to be evaluated, and the moment/context in which the process takes place. For each instance, the annotation outcome depends on these three elements, assuming the task is properly defined, designed, and carried out, e.g., in terms of quality control. We summarize these potential sources of disagreement as follows:

Individual Differences. World perception is a personal and intrinsically private experience. To some extent, this experience can be traced back to a common ground, but margins of subjectivity remain. These margins are relatively limited when they concern matters of fact, but they snowball when opinions, values, and sentiments come into play. In NLP, many annotation tasks rely on personal opinions and judgment, despite uniform instructions for annotators. For example, in hate speech detection or sentiment analysis, different annotators might have very different perspectives regarding what is hateful or negative, respectively. Individual differences remarkably influence the annotation outcome and, therefore, the disagreement levels. Such individual differences can be partially explained by cultural and socio-demographic norms and variables, such as age, gender, instruction level, or cultural background. However, none of them is sufficient to capture the uniqueness of each subject and their evaluations.

Stimulus Characteristics. Instance characteristics have paramount importance for the annotation as well. Language meaning is often equivocal and carries ambiguities of several kinds: lexical, syntactical, semantic, and others. Humour, for example, often relies on lexical or syntactic ambiguity (Raskin, 1985; Poesio, 2020). Other genres using deliberate ambiguity as a rhetorical device include poetry (Su, 1994) or political discourse (Winkler, 2015).

For some instances, more than one label is correct, and the relative annotation task would be better framed as multi-label multi-class, rather than as multi-class *tout-court*. This is a common scenario in image and text tagging, where several object/features/topics can be present: this layer of complexity is a further potential source of disagreement between coders.

Context. Last but not least, the context matters. The same coder could give different answers at different times to the same questions. The answers change as the subjects' state of mind does, and even factors such as attention slips play a non-negligible role (Beigman Klebanov et al., 2008). This lack of consistency in human behavior is well known and explored in longitudinal studies, not only in psychology but also in linguistics (Lin and Chen, 2020).

These three aspects suggest that squeezing the human experience and resulting annotation into a set of crisp variables is a gross oversimplification in most cases.

2.2 Disagreement in 'Objective' Tasks

The NLP community has long been aware that it makes no sense to evaluate natural language generation applications against a hypothetical 'gold' output. These areas have developed specialized training and evaluation methods (Papineni et al., 2002; Lin, 2004). More surprisingly, disagreements in interpretation have been found to be frequent in annotation projects concerned with apparently more 'objective' aspects of language, such as coreference (Poesio and Artstein, 2005; Recasens et al., 2011), part-of-speech tagging (Plank et al., 2014), word sense disambiguation (Passonneau et al., 2012) and semantic role labelling (Dumitrache et al., 2019), to name a few examples. Even if in these tasks individual instances can be found to be reasonably objective, these findings appear to reflect the existence of extensive and systematic disagreement on what can be concluded from a natural language statement (Pavlick and Kwiatkowski, 2019).

2.3 Disagreement on 'Subjective' Tasks

Disagreement in annotation has been studied from a particular angle when occurring in highly subjective tasks such as offensive and abusive language detection or hate speech detection. Akhtar et al. (2019) introduced the *polarization index*, aiming at measuring a particular form of disagreement stemming from clusters of annotators whose opinions on the subjective phenomenon are polarized, e.g., because of different cultural backgrounds. Specifically, polarization measures the ratio between intra-group and inter-group agreement at the individual instance level, capturing the cases where different groups of annotators strongly agree on different labels. In this view, polarization is a somewhat complementary concept to disagreement, whereas a set of annotations could exhibit the latter but not the former, or both. Akhtar et al. (2020) employs this polarization measure to extract alternative gold standards from a dataset annotated with hate speech and train multiple models in order to encode different perspectives on this highly subjective task. While it clearly appears that involving the victims of hate speech in the annotation process helps uncovering implicit manifestations of hatred, the study also shows that the plurality of perspectives is more informative than the mere sum of the annotations.

3 Evaluation in Light of Disagreement

While the research mentioned in the previous section questions the assumption that a single 'hard' label (a gold label) exists for every item in a dataset, the models proposed for learning from multiple interpretations are still largely evaluated under this assumption, using 'hard' measures like Accuracy or class-weighted F1 (Plank et al., 2014; Rodrigues and Pereira, 2018).

Abandoning the gold standard assumption requires the ability to evaluate a system's output also over instances on which annotators disagree. There is no consensus yet on this form of evaluation, but a few proposals have been used already.

In fact, a way of performing soft evaluation exists which is a natural extension of current practice in NLP. This is to evaluate ambiguity-aware models by treating the probability distribution of labels they produce as a **soft label**, and comparing that to a full distribution of labels, instead of a 'one-hot' approach. This can be done using, for example, cross-entropy, although other options also exist. This approach was adopted in, *inter alia*, (Peterson et al., 2019; Uma et al., 2020; Fornaciari et al., 2021). Peterson et al. (2019) tested this approach on image classification tasks, generating the soft label by transforming the item annotation distribution using standard normalization. Uma et al. (2020) employed this form of soft metric evaluation for NLP, also comparing different ways to obtain a soft label from the raw data. They use soft metrics to compare the classifiers' distribution to the human-derived label distributions, complementing traditional hard evaluation measures.

Basile (2020) suggested a more extreme evaluation framework, where a model is required to produce different outputs encoding the individual annotators' labels. The predictions are then individually evaluated against the single annotations, rather than against an aggregated gold standard. This proposal aims at fostering the design of 'inclusive' models with respect to diverse backgrounds in highly subjective tasks.

While evaluating with disagreement is not yet widely adopted, methods for doing so exist. In the rest of this section, we discuss the two aforementioned approaches more in detail.

3.1 The SEMEVAL 2021 Campaign

The objective of SEMEVAL-2021 Task 12 on Learning with Disagreements (LeWiDi) (Uma et al., 2021) was to provide a unified testing framework for learning from disagreements in NLP and CV using datasets containing information about disagreements for interpreting language and classifying images.

Five well-known datasets for very different NLP and CV tasks were identified, all characterized by a multiplicity of labels for each instance, by having a size sufficient to train state-of-the-art models, and by evincing different characteristics in terms of the crowd annotators and data collection procedure. These include: a dataset of Twitter posts annotated with POS tags collected by Gimpel et al. (2011), a datasets for humour identification by Simpson et al. (2019), and two CV datasets on object identification namely the LabelMe (Russell et al., 2008) and CIFAR-10 datasets (Peterson et al., 2019).

Both hard evaluation metrics (F1) and soft evaluation metrics (cross-entropy, as discussed in Section 3) were used for evaluation (Uma et al., 2021). The results showed that in nearly all cases, models that account for noise and disagreement have the best (lowest) cross-entropy scores. These results are consistent with the findings of Uma et al. (2020) and Peterson et al. (2019).

3.2 Evaluation of Highly Subjective Tasks

Basile (2020) explored the impact of disagreement caused by polarization on evaluation, focusing on NLP tasks with high levels of subjectivity. They argue that aggregated test sets lead to unfair evaluation concerning the multiple perspectives stemming from the annotator's background. Therefore, they argue for a paradigm shift in NLP evaluation, where benchmarks for highly subjective tasks should consider the diverging opinions of the annotators throughout the entire evaluation pipeline.

This proposal is tested with a simulation on synthetic data, where the annotation is conditioned on two input parameters: difficulty (as in general ambiguity of the annotation task) and subjectivity (an annotation bias linked to a predetermined background variable for the annotators). They propose a straightforward evaluation framework that accounts for multiple perspectives on highly subjective phenomena, where multiple models are trained on the annotations provided by individual annotators, and their accuracy is averaged as a final evaluation metric. The findings from the experiment show that subjectivity and ambiguity are discernible signals, as discussed in Section 2. Moreover, it is shown how a perspective-aware framework provides a more stable evaluation for classifiers of highly subjective tasks, very much in line with the results by Uma et al. (2020).

4 Conclusion

In this position paper, we argue against the current prevalent evaluation practice of comparing against a single truth. This method has allowed automated evaluation, sped up model selection and development, and resulted in good evaluation scores. However, those scores hide the truth about the state of our models: many tasks are complex and subjective. Assuming a single truth for the sake of evaluation amounts to a gross oversimplification of inherently complex matters. We further reject the notion that we should remove annotation noise from datasets. Instead, we propose to embrace the complex and subjective nature of task labels. We show how disagreement from the annotator, the data, and the context, affects even seemingly objective tasks. Research already shows that incorporating this disagreement leads to better training performance. We suggest that it can do the same for evaluation. The datasets already exist, all we need is to use them. It might not produce the same nice high scores we have gotten used to. But it will provide an honest assessment of how good our models are, and do justice to the complexity of the subject we are trying to model.

Acknowledgements

This research was supported in part by the DALI project, ERC Grant 695662, and the European Union's Horizon 2020 research and innovation program (grant agreement No. 949944, INTEGRATOR) and by the Independent Research Fund Denmark (DFF) grants No. 9131-00019B and 9063-00077B. TF and DH are members of the MilaNLP group, and the Data and Marketing Insights Unit of the Bocconi Institute for Data Science and Analysis.

References

Sohail Akhtar, Valerio Basile, and Viviana Patti. 2019. A new measure of polarization in the annotation of hate speech. In *AI*IA 2019 – Advances in Artificial Intelligence*, pages 588–603, Cham. Springer International Publishing.

Sohail Akhtar, Valerio Basile, and Viviana Patti. 2020. Modeling annotator perspective and polarized opinions to improve hate speech detection. *Proceedings of the AAAI Conference on Human Computation and Crowdsourcing*, 8(1):151–154.

Jacopo Amidei, Paul Piwek, and Alistair Willis. 2018. Rethinking the agreement in human evaluation tasks. In *Proceedings of the 27th International Conference on Computational Linguistics*, pages 3318–3329, Santa Fe, New Mexico, USA. Association for Computational Linguistics.

Lora Aroyo and Chris Welty. 2015. Truth is a lie: Crowd truth and the seven myths of human annotation. *AI Magazine*, 36(1):15–24.

Ron Artstein and Massimo Poesio. 2008. Survey article: Inter-coder agreement for computational linguistics. *Computational Linguistics*, 34(4):555–596.

Valerio Basile. 2020. It's the end of the gold standard as we know it. on the impact of pre-aggregation on the evaluation of highly subjective tasks. In *Proc. of the AIXIA Workshop*. Universitá di Torino.

Beata Beigman Klebanov and Eyal Beigman. 2009. Squibs: From annotator agreement to noise models. *Computational Linguistics*, 35(4):495–503.

Beata Beigman Klebanov, Eyal Beigman, and Daniel Diermeier. 2008. Analyzing disagreements. In *Coling 2008: Proceedings of the workshop on Human Judgements in Computational Linguistics*, pages 2–7, Manchester, UK. Coling 2008 Organizing Committee.

Samuel R Bowman and George E Dahl. 2021. What will it take to fix benchmarking in natural language understanding? *arXiv preprint arXiv:2104.02145*.

Cristina Butnariu, Su Nam Kim, Preslav Nakov, Diarmuid Ó Séaghdha, Stan Szpakowicz, and Tony Veale. 2009. SemEval-2010 task 9: The interpretation of noun compounds using paraphrasing verbs and prepositions. In *Proceedings of the Workshop on Semantic Evaluations: Recent Achievements and Future Directions (SEW-2009)*, pages 100–105, Boulder, Colorado. Association for Computational Linguistics.

Kenneth Ward Church and Joel Hestness. 2019. A survey of 25 years of evaluation. *Natural Language Engineering*, 25(6):753–767.

Anca Dumitrache, Lora Aroyo, and Chris Welty. 2019. A crowdsourced frame disambiguation corpus with ambiguity. In *Proceedings of the 2019 Conference of the North American Chapter of the Association for Computational Linguistics: Human Language Technologies, Volume 1 (Long and Short Papers)*, pages 2164–2170, Minneapolis, Minnesota. Association for Computational Linguistics.

Tommaso Fornaciari, Silviu Uma, Alexandra Paun, Barbara Plank, Dirk Hovy, and Massimo Poesio. 2021. Beyond black & white: Leveraging annotator disagreement via soft-label multi-task learning. In *Proceedings of the 2021 Conference of the North American Chapter of the Association for Computational Linguistics: Human Language Technologies, Volume 1 (Long and Short Papers)*. Association for Computational Linguistics.

Kevin Gimpel, Nathan Schneider, Brendan O'Connor, Dipanjan Das, Daniel Mills, Jacob Eisenstein, Michael Heilman, Dani Yogatama, Jeffrey Flanigan, and Noah A. Smith. 2011. Part-of-speech tagging for Twitter: Annotation, features, and experiments. In *Proceedings of the 49th Annual Meeting of the Association for Computational Linguistics: Human Language Technologies*, pages 42–47, Portland, Oregon, USA. Association for Computational Linguistics.

Yash Goyal, Tejas Khot, Douglas Summers-Stay, Dhruv Batra, and Devi Parikh. 2017. Making the V in VQA matter: Elevating the role of image understanding in Visual Question Answering. In *Conference on Computer Vision and Pattern Recognition (CVPR)*.

Iris Hendrickx, Zornitsa Kozareva, Preslav Nakov, Diarmuid Ó Séaghdha, Stan Szpakowicz, and Tony Veale. 2013. SemEval-2013 task 4: Free paraphrases of noun compounds. In *Second Joint Conference on Lexical and Computational Semantics (*SEM), Volume 2: Proceedings of the Seventh International Workshop on Semantic Evaluation (SemEval 2013)*, pages 138–143, Atlanta, Georgia, USA. Association for Computational Linguistics.

Dirk Hovy, Taylor Berg-Kirkpatrick, Ashish Vaswani, and Eduard Hovy. 2013. Learning whom to trust with MACE. In *Proceedings of the 2013 Conference of the North American Chapter of the Association for Computational Linguistics: Human Language Technologies*, pages 1120–1130, Atlanta, Georgia. Association for Computational Linguistics.

Nancy Ide and James Pustejovsky, editors. 2017. *The Handbook of Linguistic Annotation*. Springer.

Emily Jamison and Iryna Gurevych. 2015. Noise or additional information? leveraging crowdsource annotation item agreement for natural language tasks. In *Proceedings of the 2015 Conference on Empirical Methods in Natural Language Processing*, pages 291–297, Lisbon, Portugal. Association for Computational Linguistics.

David Jurgens. 2013. Embracing ambiguity: A comparison of annotation methodologies for crowdsourcing word sense labels. In *Proceedings of the 2013 Conference of the North American Chapter of the Association for Computational Linguistics: Human Language Technologies*, pages 556–562, Atlanta, Georgia. Association for Computational Linguistics.

Kian Kenyon-Dean, Eisha Ahmed, Scott Fujimoto, Jeremy Georges-Filteau, Christopher Glasz, Barleen Kaur, Auguste Lalande, Shruti Bhanderi, Robert Belfer, Nirmal Kanagasabai, Roman Sarrazingendron, Rohit Verma, and Derek Ruths. 2018. Sentiment analysis: It's complicated! In *Proceedings of the 2018 Conference of the North American Chapter of the Association for Computational Linguistics: Human Language Technologies, Volume 1 (Long Papers)*, pages 1886–1895, New Orleans, Louisiana. Association for Computational Linguistics.

Chin-Yew Lin. 2004. ROUGE: A package for automatic evaluation of summaries. In *Text Summarization Branches Out*, pages 74–81, Barcelona, Spain. Association for Computational Linguistics.

You-Min Lin and Michelle Y. Chen. 2020. Understanding writing quality change: A longitudinal study of repeaters of a high-stakes standardized english proficiency test. *Language Testing*, 37(4):523–549.

Kishore Papineni, Salim Roukos, Todd Ward, and Wei-Jing Zhu. 2002. Bleu: a method for automatic evaluation of machine translation. In *Proceedings of the 40th Annual Meeting of the Association for Computational Linguistics*, pages 311–318, Philadelphia, Pennsylvania, USA. Association for Computational Linguistics.

Rebecca J. Passonneau, Vikas Bhardwaj, Ansaf Salleb-Aouissi, and Nancy Ide. 2012. Multiplicity and word sense: evaluating and learning from multiply labeled word sense annotations. *Language Resources and Evaluation*, 46(2):219–252.

Rebecca J. Passonneau and Bob Carpenter. 2013. The benefits of a model of annotation. In *Proceedings of the 7th Linguistic Annotation Workshop and Interoperability with Discourse*, pages 187–195, Sofia, Bulgaria. Association for Computational Linguistics.

Silviu Paun, Bob Carpenter, Jon Chamberlain, Dirk Hovy, Udo Kruschwitz, and Massimo Poesio. 2018. Comparing Bayesian models of annotation. *Transactions of the Association for Computational Linguistics*, 6:571–585.

Ellie Pavlick and Tom Kwiatkowski. 2019. Inherent disagreements in human textual inferences. *Transactions of the Association for Computational Linguistics*, 7:677–694.

Joshua C. Peterson, Ruairidh M. Battleday, Thomas L. Griffiths, and Olga Russakovsky. 2019. Human uncertainty makes classification more robust. *2019 IEEE/CVF International Conference on Computer Vision (ICCV)*, pages 9616–9625.

Barbara Plank, Dirk Hovy, and Anders Søgaard. 2014. Linguistically debatable or just plain wrong? In *Proceedings of the 52nd Annual Meeting of the Association for Computational Linguistics (Volume 2: Short Papers)*, pages 507–511, Baltimore, Maryland. Association for Computational Linguistics.

Massimo Poesio. 2020. Ambiguity. In Daniel Gutzmann, Lisa Matthewson, and Cécile Meier and Hotze Rullmann and Thomas Ede Zimmermann, editors, *The Companion to Semantics*. Wiley.

Massimo Poesio and Ron Artstein. 2005. The reliability of anaphoric annotation, reconsidered: Taking ambiguity into account. In *Proc. of ACL Workshop on Frontiers in Corpus Annotation*, pages 76–83.

Victor Raskin. 1985. *Semantic Mechanisms of Humor*. D. Reidel, Dordrecht and Boston.

Marta Recasens, Ed Hovy, and M. Antonia Martí. 2011. Identity, non-identity, and near-identity: Addressing the complexity of coreference. *Lingua*, 121(6):1138–1152.

Philip Resnik and Jimmy Lin. 2010. 11 evaluation of nlp systems. *The handbook of computational linguistics and natural language processing*, 57.

Filipe Rodrigues and Francisco C. Pereira. 2018. Deep learning from crowds. In *AAAI Conference on Artificial Intelligence*.

Bryan C. Russell, Antonio Torralba, Kevin P. Murphy, and William T. Freeman. 2008. LabelMe: A database and Web-based tool for image annotation. *International Journal of Computer Vision*, 77:157–173.

Edwin Simpson, Erik-Lân Do Dinh, Tristan Miller, and Iryna Gurevych. 2019. Predicting humorousness and metaphor novelty with Gaussian process preference learning. In *Proceedings of the 57th Annual Meeting of the Association for Computational Linguistics*, pages 5716–5728, Florence, Italy. Association for Computational Linguistics.

Soon P. Su. 1994. *Lexical Ambiguity in Poetry*. Longman, London.

Alexandra Uma, Tommaso Fornaciari, Anca Dumitrache, Tristan Miller, Jon Chamberlain, Barbara Plank, and Massimo Poesio. 2021. Semeval-2021 task 12: Learning with disagreements. In *Proceedings of the Fifteenth Workshop on Semantic Evaluation*. Association for Computational Linguistics.

Alexandra Uma, Tommaso Fornaciari, Dirk Hovy, Silviu Paun, Barbara Plank, and Massimo Poesio. 2020. A case for soft-loss functions. In *Proceedings of the 8th AAAI Conference on Human Computation and Crowdsourcing*, pages 173–177.

Chris van der Lee, Albert Gatt, Emiel van Miltenburg, Sander Wubben, and Emiel Krahmer. 2019. Best practices for the human evaluation of automatically generated text. In *Proceedings of the 12th International Conference on Natural Language Generation*, pages 355–368, Tokyo, Japan. Association for Computational Linguistics.

Susanne Winkler, editor. 2015. *Ambiguity: Language and Communication*. De Gruyter.

How Might We Create Better Benchmarks for Speech Recognition?

Alëna Aksënova
Google
New York City, USA
alenaks@google.com

Daan van Esch
Google
Amsterdam, NL
dvanesch@google.com

James Flynn
Google
New York City, USA
jpflynn@google.com

Pavel Golik
Google
New York City, USA
golik@google.com

Abstract

The applications of automatic speech recognition (ASR) systems are proliferating, in part due to recent significant quality improvements. However, as recent work indicates, even state-of-the-art speech recognition systems – some which deliver impressive benchmark results, struggle to generalize across use cases. We review relevant work, and, hoping to inform future benchmark development, outline a taxonomy of speech recognition use cases, proposed for the next generation of ASR benchmarks. We also survey work on metrics, in addition to the de facto standard Word Error Rate (WER) metric, and we introduce a versatile framework designed to describe interactions between linguistic variation and ASR performance metrics.

1 Introduction

The applications of ASR systems are many and varied; conversational virtual assistants on smartphones and smart-home devices, automatic captioning for videos, text dictation, and phone chat bots for customer support, to name a few. This proliferation has been enabled by significant gains in ASR quality. ASR quality is typically measured by *word error rate* (WER), or, informally, the Levenshtein distance between the target transcript and the machine-generated transcript (Levenshtein, 1966; Wang et al., 2003)—see Section 3.

Current state-of-the-art accuracy is now in low-single-digits for the widely used Librispeech benchmark set (Panayotov et al., 2015), with e.g. Zhang et al. (2020) achieving a WER of 1.4%. However, as Szymański et al. (2020) have pointed out, overall, our current ASR benchmarks leave much to be desired when it comes to evaluating performance across multiple real-world applications. Typical benchmark sets beyond Librispeech include TIMIT (Garofolo et al., 1993), Switchboard (Godfrey et al., 1992), WSJ (Paul and Baker, 1992), CALLHOME (Canavan et al., 1997), and Fisher (Cieri et al., 2004).[1] These benchmark sets cover a range of speech use cases, including read speech (e.g. Librispeech), and spontaneous speech (e.g. Switchboard).

However, with many ASR systems benchmarking in the low single digits, small improvements have become increasingly difficult to interpret, and any remaining errors may be concentrated. For example, for Switchboard, a considerable portion of the remaining errors involve filler words, hesitations and non-verbal backchannel cues (Xiong et al., 2017; Saon et al., 2017).

Furthermore, achieving state-of-the-art results on one of these sets does not necessarily mean that an ASR system will generalize successfully when faced with input from a wide range of domains at inference time: as Likhomanenko et al. (2020) show, "no single validation or test set from public datasets is sufficient to measure transfer to other public datasets or to real-world audio data". In one extreme example, Keung et al. (2020) show that modern ASR architectures may even start emitting repetitive, nonsensical transcriptions when faced with audio from a domain that was not covered at training time—even in cases where it would have achieved perfectly acceptable Librispeech evaluation numbers. Inspired by Goodhart's law, which states that any measure that becomes a target ceases to be a good measure, we argue that as a field, it behooves us to think more about better benchmarks in order to gain a well-rounded view of the performance of ASR systems across domains.

In this paper, we make three contributions. First, we provide a taxonomy of relevant domains, based on our experience developing ASR systems for use in many different products, with the goal of helping make next-generation benchmarks as representative as possible (Biber, 1993). Second, we argue that optimizing only for WER, as most current benchmarks imply, does not reflect considerations that are ubiquitous in real-world deployments of ASR technology: for example, pro-

[1] For an overview of such datasets and benchmarks, see https://github.com/syhw/wer_are_we. Additionally, FAIR recently released the Casual Conversations dataset intended for AI fairness measurements (Hazirbas et al., 2021).

Proceedings of the 1st Workshop on Benchmarking: Past, Present and Future, pages 22–34
August 5–6, 2021. ©2021 Association for Computational Linguistics

duction considerations such as latency and compute resources can imply additional interrelated optimization objectives. We survey relevant work on additional metrics that can be used to measure ASR systems. Third, we describe what metadata would be useful in next-generation benchmark data sets in order to help analyze the interaction between linguistic variation and performance of ASR systems—for example, to measure how well an ASR system holds up in the face of sociolinguistic variation within the target language, or second-language accents, as in e.g. Feng et al. (2021).

2 ASR Use Cases

With ASR use cases spanning many applications and tasks, ideally ASR systems would be robust to various classes of variation in speech input. For example, an ASR system which provides automatic captions for video meetings would recognize words from many different semantic fields, adaptable to the topic of the meeting. Speech characteristics may also vary across domains: for example, the speech style used when dictating text messages differs from the style of a group conversation, where speakers may occasionally talk over each other.

An ideal benchmark set would include what we will call 'horizontal' and 'vertical' variation. Horizontal challenges refer to a wide variety of scenarios where ASR may be used, while vertical challenges involve e.g. diversity in topics, encoding formats, and others.

2.1 Horizontals: ASR applications

ASR application domains can be roughly subdivided based on the number of speakers, the mode of speech (spontaneous vs. prepared speech) and the intended recipient (human or device). An ideal benchmark set would cover as many of these horizontals as possible—e.g. through merging existing benchmark sets, as does Likhomanenko et al. (2020), and adding additional data to cover any gaps.

Dictation *Text dictation* is a popular use case of ASR systems — one of the first successful commercial applications with broad appeal. This feature serves both convenience and accessibility, allowing users to enter text without manually typing. Dictation tends to involve relatively slow speech, typically that of a single speaker, who is aware they are interacting with a device, and who may consciously modify their speech patterns to facilitate device understanding (Cohn et al., 2020). Dictation may have applications in many fields. One with many idiosyncratic challenges is *medical dictation*, where ASR systems are used to help medical personnel take notes and generate medical records (Miner et al., 2020; Mani et al., 2020). This poses challenges in the support of domain-specific jargon, which we will discuss in subsection 2.2. In a related application, *dictation practice* is sometimes used by language learners, often in combination with a pronunciation feedback system (McCrocklin, 2019). In other contexts, transcription of dictated audio may be part of a composite pipeline, such as in *automatic translation*, where the initial transcript feeds a subsequent system for translation to another language.

Voice Search and Control *Voice search* and other *conversational assistant* products enable users to access information or invoke actions via spoken input. Similar to dictation, audio in such settings is typically single-speaker, with human-to-device characteristics. Compared to dictation, queries may be somewhat shorter, and may contain proper nouns (e.g. place names or business names). Semiotic-class tokens such as times (Sproat et al., 2001) are also more common in this setting. A related type of human-to-device speech is *interactive voice response (IVR)*, where callers to customer support may first interact with a voice chatbot, which can help gather information prior to redirecting the call, or potentially resolve issues itself. (Inam et al., 2017).

Voicemails, Oration, and Audiobooks While dictation users may modify their speech based on the knowledge that they are dictating directly to a device, ASR systems may also be used to help provide transcriptions for voicemail messages (Padmanabhan et al., 2002; Liao et al., 2010), parliamentary speeches (Gollan et al., 2005; Steingrímsson et al., 2020), and so on. Such settings, while still typically single-speaker, include artifacts of spontaneity—e.g. fillers or hesitations like 'uh', backchannel speech, as well as disfluencies, false starts, and corrections (Jamshid Lou and Johnson, 2020; Mendelev et al., 2021; Knudsen et al., 2020). Transcribing *audiobooks* includes elements of dictation and oration: due to their read-speech nature, audiobooks typically contain less spontaneity than typical human-to-human speech (Igras-Cybulska et al.), but they are usually more natural than human-to-device speech.[2]

Conversations and Meetings In settings such as *human-to-human conversations*, the task of the ASR system typically involves transcribing spontaneous speech among several participants within a single audio recording. For example, *meeting transcription*

[2]Transcription of audiobooks is a primary goal of Librispeech (Panayotov et al., 2015), one of the most common benchmarks for ASR today, even though practically speaking, transcribing audiobook audio is not a common task for most real-world ASR systems—given that audiobooks are typically produced based on an existing 'transcription', namely the ground-truth written text of the book.

can help to improve accessibility of video meetings, or may serve to document conversations (Kanda et al., 2021); see e.g. Janin et al. (2004); Carletta et al. (2005) for relevant data sets. Another use case for transcriptions of human-to-human conversations is *customer-agent conversations*, as well as other types of *telephony*, which can help monitor the quality of phone-based customer service.

Podcasts, Movies and TV *Podcast transcription* forms a related, and fast-growing, application area, with recent data sets including Clifton et al. (2020). Podcast transcription is in some ways similar to the long-standing task of automatically transcribing *interviews*, e.g. to help make them more accessible, as in various oral-history projects (Byrne et al., 2004). Finally, another similar use case is the transcription of motion pictures, including documentaries, which may require increased robustness to non-speech audio, such as music and special effects. Spontaneous speech is common to these human-to-human, multi-speaker settings, with fillers such as 'uh', overlap, and interruption between speakers. We draw a distinction between movie subtitling and TV closed captioning. Subtitling is an 'offline' task in that the entire audio is available to the ASR system at recognition time, and the setting allows for multiple passes, including human post-editors. Compare to closed captioning, where streaming ASR processes a live broadcast with tight latency constraints. Additionally, these two modes have different transcription conventions and formatting requirements. Subtitles often contain non-verbal cues that support comprehension for hearing impaired, and are optimized for readability. Conversely, closed captions are often projected in upper case with fewer constraints, such as line breaks, to denote speaker turns.

2.2 Verticals: Technical challenges

ASR applications do not just differ in the style of speech. Other dimensions include: the semantic content of the input speech (a lecture about nuclear physics involves very different terminology than a phone conversation to set up a car maintenance appointment), the audio encoding format, and sample rate, among others. Again, the *ideal* benchmark should cover as many of these factors as possible.

Terminology and Phrases ASR systems applied to a wide range of domains need to recognize hundreds of thousands, if not millions, of distinct words. Such systems typically involve a language model trained on large volumes of text from multiple sources. To benchmark an ASR system's capability across a wide range of topics, test sets could include terms and phrases from many different fields: consider medical terminology (e.g. 'ribonucleotides'), historical phrases (e.g. 'Yotvingians'), and many more. ASR systems should also be savvy to neologisms (e.g. 'doomscrolling'), although, admittedly, the fast-changing nature of neologisms and trending phrases makes this particularly challenging. Another area that deserves special attention in measurements is loanwords, which may have pronunciations that involve unusual grapheme-to-phoneme correspondences; such words may even necessitate personalized pronunciation learning (Bruguier et al., 2016).

Speed Recordings where speech is significantly faster or slower than average may pose additional recognition challenges (Siegler and Stern, 1995; Fosler-Lussier and Morgan, 1999), so the ideal benchmark should also cover samples with various speech rates. This is particularly important for paid services, where users sometimes artificially speed up the recordings or cut out easily detectable portions of silence in order to reduce costs. Such processing can introduce unnatural shifts in pitch and add confusion to the punctuation at speaker turn, and sentence boundaries.

Acoustic Environment The setting in which the input audio was recorded (real-life or phone conversation, video call, dictation) can also materially impact ASR performance, and settings with high amounts of background noise can be particularly challenging. Ideally, test sets should be available to measure how robust an ASR system is in the face of background noise and other environmental factors (Park et al., 2019; Kinoshita et al., 2020). The entertainment domain contains a large amount of scenes with background music, which often have lyrics that are usually not meant to be transcribed. Even call center conversations sometimes contain hold music which is not part of the payload of the call.

Encoding Formats Lastly, different audio encodings (linear PCM, A-law, μ-law), codecs (FLAC, OPUS, MP3) and non-standard sample rates such as 17 kHz may affect recognition quality, and should be represented (Sanderson and Paliwal, 1997; Hokking et al., 2016). The same holds for audio that has been up- or down-sampled, e.g. between 8 kHz typical for telephony and 16 kHz or above, for broadcast media.

2.3 Practical Issues

We argue that the more horizontal and vertical areas are covered by a benchmark, the more representative it will be, and hence the more appropriate for measuring ASR progress. There are some practical matters that are also important to consider when creating the ideal benchmark.

Transcription Conventions Creating transcriptions of human speech in a consistent manner can be unexpectedly challenging: for example, should hesitations like 'uh' be transcribed? How should transcribers handle unusual cases like the artist 'dead mouse', which is written as 'deadmau5' by convention? And if a speaker says 'wanna', should the transcription reflect that as such, or should the transcriber transcribe that as 'want to'? The answer to such questions will depend on the downstream use context (e.g. a dialog system, where hesitations may be useful, or an email message, where they may need to be omitted instead). For example, while in closed captioning or podcast transcriptions omitting repetitions, disfluencies, and filler words (e.g. "like", "kind of") is considered desirable, this might not be appropriate for some other ASR domains such as subtitling. Defining and applying a comprehensive set of transcription conventions, as e.g. Switchboard (Godfrey et al., 1992) and CORAAL (Kendall and Farrington, 2020), is critical in building high-quality data sets. It is also important to detect and correct transcription errors in annotated corpora (Rosenberg, 2012).

Perhaps the most important choice in such transcription conventions is whether to adopt 'spoken-domain' transcriptions, where numbers are spelled out in words (e.g. 'three thirty'), or 'written-domain' transcriptions, where they are rendered in the typical written form ('3:30'). Many data sets use spoken-domain transcriptions only, but often in real-world ASR deployments it is valuable for readability and downstream usage (e.g. by a natural-language understanding system), to have fully-formatted, written-domain transcripts, as described by O'Neill et al. (2021)—who also provide a written-domain benchmark data set.

Representativeness For any ASR test set, at least two considerations come into play: first, how closely does the test set approximate reality; and second, is the test set sufficiently large to be representative? For example, test sets that are intended to measure how well an ASR system deals with speech with background noise should have a realistic amount of background noise: not too little, but also not too much—e.g. to the point that even human listeners stand no chance of transcribing the audio correctly. Adding noise artificially, as established e.g. by the Aurora corpora (Pearce and Hirsch, 2000; Parihar and Picone, 2002), does not take into account the Lombard effect. In terms of size, analyses akin to Guyon et al. (1998) are helpful to ensure that any change is statistically significant; we are not aware of much work along these lines for ASR systems specifically, but it seems like it would be worthwhile to explore this area more. The ultimate goal should be to increase the predictive power of error metrics.

3 Metrics: WER and Beyond

Assume, for the sake of argument, that an impressive selection of test sets has been collected in order to create our imagined ideal next-generation benchmark for ASR, covering many use cases, technical challenges, and so on. The performance of an ASR system could now be measured simply by computing a single, overall WER across all the utterances in this collection of test sets—and a system that yields lower WER on this benchmark could be said to be 'better' than a system with higher WER.

However, in a real-world deployment setting, the question of which system is 'best' typically relies on an analysis of many metrics. For example, imagine a system with a WER of 1.5% but an average transcription latency of 2500 milliseconds, and another system that achieves 1.6% WER but a latency of only 1250 milliseconds: in many settings, the second system could still be more suitable for deployment, despite achieving worse WER results. Of course, 'latency' itself is not a well-defined term: sometimes the measurement is reported as the average delay between the end of each spoken word and the time it is emitted by the ASR system, while in other cases the measure is based only on the first or the last word in an utterance. Neither is well-defined in presence of recognition errors. Yet another kind of latency is end-to-end latency, involving everything between the microphone activity and the final projection of results, including network overhead and optional post-processing like capitalization, punctuation etc. A "pure" ASR latency metric ignores those and focuses on the processing time of the recognizer, while latency in the context of voice assistant commands may consider the delay before successful recognition of a command, which might sometimes precede the actual end of utterance. In this section, we describe how, much like latency, even WER itself has many nuances, and we point to other metrics, beyond WER and latency, that can be considered account when measuring ASR systems.

3.1 WER

The workhorse metric of ASR is the Word Error Rate, or WER. Calculating WER is relatively easy on spoken-domain transcriptions with no formatting (e.g. 'set an alarm for seven thirty') but quickly becomes a nuanced matter when processing written-domain transcriptions—for example, if the ground truth is provided as 'Set an alarm for 7:30.' with capitalization and punctuation, is it an error in WER terms if the system emits lowercase 'set' instead of uppercase 'Set', as given in the ground truth? Typically, for standard WER calculations in such scenarios, capitalization and word-final punctuation is not considered to be a factor, and other metrics are calculated for fully-formatted WER—e.g. case-sensitive WER, where 'set' vs 'Set' would be considered an error.

WER can also be calculated on only a subset of relevant words or phrases: for example, it may be helpful to compute separate error rates for different kinds of semiotic classes, such as spoken punctuation, times, or phone numbers—as well as for different semantic areas, such as relevant domain terminology vs. generic English words. The assessment of ASR quality on rare phrases is yet another issue—average WER does not always adequately reflect how well an ASR system picks up rare yet important words, suggesting it may be valuable to know WER for common and less common words. A related approach is to use precision-recall, e.g. as Chiu et al. (2018) do for medical terminology. Such 'sliced' approaches can help provide insight into the recognition quality of words or phrases that are particularly salient in a given setting. For example, if a system that is intended for use in a voicemail transcription setting achieves 3% overall WER, but it mistranscribes every phone number, that system would almost certainly not be preferred over a system that achieves 3.5% overall WER, but that makes virtually no mistakes on phone numbers. As Peyser et al. (2019) show, such examples are far from theoretical; fortunately, as they show, it is also possible to create synthetic test sets using text-to-speech systems to get a sense of WER in a specific context. Standard tools like NIST SCLITE[3] can be used to calculate WER and various additional statistics.

Importantly, it is possible to calculate the local WER on any level of granularity: utterance, speaker turn, file, entire recording etc. The *average* WER alone, weighted by the number of words, is not sufficient to describe the shape of the distribution over the individual local measurements. Given two ASR systems with identical WERs, we almost always prefer the one with the lower standard deviation, as it reduces the uncertainty w.r.t. the worst case. A more accurate metric that samples the shape of the distribution consists of percentiles (e.g. 90, 95 or 99) that are more suitable to provide an upper bound. Additionally, reporting the standard deviation allows researchers to judge whether an improvement in WER is significant or just a statistical fluctuation. The same argument holds true for latency.

Finally, WER can also be calculated on not just the top machine hypothesis, but also on the full *n-best* list, as in e.g. Biadsy et al. (2017).

[3]https://www.nist.gov/itl/iad/mig/tools

3.2 Metadata about Words

Correctly transcribing speech into text is the most critical part of an ASR system, but downstream use cases may require more than just a word-by-word textual transcription of the input audio. For example, having *per-word confidence scores* can be helpful in dialog systems (Yu et al., 2011); having accurate timestamps at the word level is essential in many application of the long form domain, such as closed captioning, subtitling and keyword search; having *phonemic transcriptions* for every word enables downstream disambiguation (e.g. when the transcription gives 'live', did the user say the adjective [lɪv] or the verb [laɪv]); and emitting *word timings* to indicate where each word appeared in the audio can be important for search applications, especially for longer recordings. The ideal ASR benchmark would also make it possible to verify this metadata: for example, if it is possible to use forced alignment to infer where in the audio words appear, and to check how accurately an ASR system is emitting word timings (Sainath et al., 2020a). *speaker diarization* is yet another type of of metadata that can be emitted at a per-word or per-phrase level, for which independent benchmarks already exist (Ryant et al., 2021).

3.3 Real-Time Factor

A general metric for the processing speed is the real-time factor (RTF), commonly defined as the ratio between the processing wall-clock time and the raw audio duration (Liu, 2000). Streaming ASR systems are required to operate at an RTF below one, but in applications that do not require immediate processing an RTF over one might be acceptable. As with WER and latency, RTF samples form a distribution, whose shape is important in understanding the behavior in the worst case. The process of finding the most likely hypothesis in ASR (often referred to as "decoding" for historical reasons) requires an efficient exploration of the search space: a subset of all possible hypotheses. The larger the search space, the slower the search, but the more likely is the recognizer to find the correct hypothesis. A small search space allows for quick decoding, but often comes at the cost of higher WER. It is common to report an RTF vs WER curve which shows all possible operating points, allowing for mutual trade off. Note this definition operates with the wall-clock time, thus ignoring the hardware requirements. It is common to normalize the RTF by the number of CPU cores and hardware accelerators.

3.4 Streaming ASR

For ASR systems that stream output to the user while recognition is ongoing, as in many voice assistant and dictation applications, additional metrics will be useful, e.g. measuring the *stability of partial results*, which reflects the number of times the recognizer changes previously emitted words while recognizing a query (Shangguan et al., 2020). A related dimension is *quality of the intermediate hypotheses*: a streaming system that emits highly inaccurate intermediate hypotheses can yield a jarring user experience, even if the final hypothesis achieves an acceptable WER. This is particularly important in combination with a downstream application like machine translation that can be very sensitive to corrections in partial hypotheses (Ansari et al., 2020).

Yet another factor is streaming latency, e.g. how quickly partials are emitted (Shangguan et al., 2021), and more generally, the delay between the end of the user's input and the finalized transcription (Sainath et al., 2020b; Yu et al., 2021). The accuracy of the *endpointer* module can significantly affect this latency: endpointers need to strike the right balance between keeping the microphone open while the user may still continue speaking (e.g. if the user pauses briefly to collect their thoughts), while closing it as soon as the user is likely to be done speaking, and a number of relevant endpointer metrics can be calculated, as in e.g. Li et al. (2020).

3.5 Inference and Training

Latency is influenced by many factors beyond the quality of the endpointer: for example, the number of parameters in the ASR model, the surrounding software stack, and the computational resources available will impact the duration of the recognition process for an audio recording, in both streaming and non-streaming - batch recognition settings. Compressing models can help them run faster, and in more settings (Peng et al., 2021), although the impact of shrinking models should be measured carefully (Hooker et al., 2020a,b).

Beyond inference, training may also be worth benchmarking in more detail: factors such as the number of parameters in the model, the model architecture, the amount of data used, the training software, and the hardware available will influence how long it takes to train an ASR model using a given algorithm. Benchmarks such as MLPerf (Mattson et al., 2020) do not yet incorporate speech recognition, but this may be worth exploring in the future.

3.6 Contextual Biasing

Certain phrases or words are sometimes expected in dialogue contexts (e.g. 'yes' or 'no'), along with particular types of words (e.g. brand names in the context of shopping). In such cases, ASR systems may allow for *contextual biasing* to increase the language model probability of relevant words or phrases (Aleksic et al., 2015). Measuring contextual biasing typically involves evaluating a relevant test set twice: once with, and once without the contextual biasing enabled (the default behavior). Even when contextual biasing is enabled, it will typically be desirable for the system to continue to recognize other words and phrases without too much of an accuracy impact, so that recognition results remain reasonable in the event that the input does not contain the words or phrases that were expected—typically anti-sets will be used, as described by Aleksic et al. (2015). Contextual biasing plays a key role in classical dialogue systems like IVR.

3.7 Hallucination

In some cases, ASR models can *hallucinate* transcriptions: e.g. providing transcriptions for audio even where no speech is present, or simply misbehaving on out-of-domain utterances (Liao et al., 2015; Keung et al., 2020). Intuitively, this type of errors should be reported explicitly as the "insertion rate", which is calculated as part of the WER anyway. However, insertion errors are rather rare and do not stand out strongly in presence of speech and natural recognition errors.

Measuring whether an ASR system is prone to such hallucinations can be done by running it on test sets from domains that were unseen at training time. In addition, it is possible to employ *reject sets* which contain various kinds of audio that should *not* result in a transcription: for example, such reject sets may cover various noises (e.g. AudioSet Gemmeke et al. (2017)), silence, speech in other languages, and so on.

A related topic is *adversarial attacks*, when a particular message is 'hidden' in audio in a way that humans cannot hear, but which may deceive ASR systems into transcribing in an unexpected way; measuring robustness to such issues would be desirable, but it remains an active area of research—much like the creation of such attacks more broadly (Carlini and Wagner, 2018).

3.8 Debuggability and Fixability

Finally, one aspect of ASR systems that tends to be important for real-world deployments, but which is hard to quantify in a numeric metric, is how easy it is to debug and fix any misrecognitions that may arise. For example, if a new word such as 'COVID-19' comes up which is not yet recognized by the system, it would be preferable if adding such a new word could be done without necessitating a full retrain of the system. While quantifying this property of ASR systems is hard, we believe that the degree to which it is easy to debug and fix any ASR system is worth mentioning.

4 Demographically Informed Quality

As previously discussed, the ideal benchmark for ASR systems would cover as many horizontals and verticals as possible, and would involve various kinds of metrics beyond just WER. Another important dimension, however, would be the availability of demographic characteristics, and analyzing the metrics based on such characteristics. Such demographic characteristics may correlate with linguistic variation—for example, non-native speakers of English may have an accent showing traces of their native language—which may in turn impact ASR performance. Having demographic characteristics can help produce analyses like the one reported by Feng et al. (2021), who analyzed differences in recognition performance for different accents, age ranges, and gender within an ASR system.

The ideal benchmark set, then, should include sufficient metadata to run similar analyses, enabling developers to understand how their system behaves when processing various accents or dialects; to see whether factors like gender and age influence recognition performance in their system. Linguistic variation may take many different shapes, including:

- phonetic differences, e.g. vowel realizations that are specific to a given accent
- phonological differences, e.g. various number of phonemes in different dialects of a language
- lexical differences, e.g. region-specific terms
- syntactical differences, e.g. double-negatives
- voice quality differences, e.g. pitch differences, which are correlated with parameters such as gender and age (Liao et al., 2015)

Fortunately, several data sets already exist with relevant demographic tags for many utterances, e.g. Mozilla Common Voice (Ardila et al., 2020) which offers public data sets across many languages with dialect and accent tags. There are also academic data sets produced by sociolinguists, such as CORAAL for AAVE (Kendall and Farrington, 2020), ESLORA for Galician Spanish (Barcala et al., 2018), the Corpus Gesproken Nederlands for Dutch (van Eerten, 2007), and others. Such corpora provide a useful blueprint for providing such metadata, and we believe that it would be valuable for similar tags to be available for as many other data set as possible. As Andrus et al. (2021) show, at times it will likely be difficult to get the demographic metadata that is needed, but still, getting such data wherever possible is important—as they put it, "what we can't measure, we can't understand".

Even where demographic information is already present in ASR evaluation sets, it can be a valuable to conduct an analysis of the target user base for a deployed ASR system in order to ensure that all relevant tags are available. For example, if a data set has labels for four distinct accents, but the target user base is known from sociolinguistic research to use six distinct accents, this gap will not necessarily be evident when running an analysis of any possible differences among the four accents for which tags are available. It is important to understand the sociolinguistic characteristics of the target user base, and to cover as many of these properties as possible. Given that language has almost infinite variation as you zoom in—in the extreme, everyone has a slightly different voice—this is a task that requires careful sociolinguistic judgement and analysis, calling for interdisciplinary collaboration between linguists and developers of ASR systems.

Even when a rich set of tags is available, it can be difficult to interpret the results. We describe a simple, metric-independent population-weighted visualization framework designed to evaluate ASR systems based on such demographic metadata. Our approach supports the different language variations outlined above, and we propose this analyses as a valuable addition to future benchmarks.

4.1 Population-Weighted Slicing Framework

Factors like accents (native or non-native), dialects, gender, and others can result in linguistic variation, and this may in turn impact ASR performance. Thus it can be valuable to calculate WER, latency, and other metrics not just on a data set as a whole, but

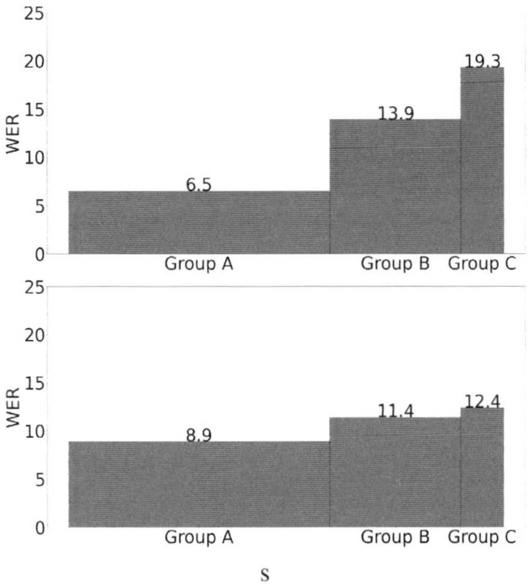

Figure 1: Examples of WER sliced into groups A, B, and C, with the width of the bars reflecting relative sizes of those groups.

also to slice metrics based on such meta-linguistic parameters.

Such sliced metrics can be used to determine any performance gap between groups, and if so, what efforts may need to be undertaken to shrink such gaps. The ideal test set should be representative of the target user base, but as this may be hard to achieve at data collection time, it can make sense to re-weight any metrics based on real-world population statistics: for example, imagine a scenario where 98% of the recordings in a data set come from native speakers, with the remaining 2% coming from non-native speakers. If the target deployment setting involves more like 15% non-native speech, the metrics obtained over the 2% slice of the data set coming from non-native speakers should carry 15% of the weight.

To make such analyses easier, we propose subdividing all speakers into mutually exclusive groups based on relevant linguistic or demographic criteria. For example, consider a scenario where the real-world population is subdivided into 3 mutually exclusive groups: group A (60% of the population), group B (30%), and group C (10%). The two subplots of Figure 1 visualize examples of evaluations of two ASR models for slices corresponding to these groups, with the WER scores represented by the height of the bars, and the width of the bars reflecting the size of the groups.

Even in the actual test data set, group A covers 80% of the test data, with groups B and C accounting for 10% each (i.e. under-representing group B and over-representing group A), this population-weighted framework provides an intuitive way to address this imbalance, and understand how ASR systems perform in the face of linguistic diversity. The average WER of the system can be calculated as an average of all WER scores across population groups, weighted according to the size of those groups—which may differ from the WER obtained by simply calculating the WER on the actual data set, as we have re-weighted based on the real-world distribution.

Importantly, while the average weighted WER is a useful metric, the full distribution should still be understood: continuing the example depicted on Figure 1, the average WER for both scenarios in this case would be 10[4], but the disparity between the various groups in the plot where group C achieves a WER of 19.3% is clearly much bigger in one scenario than another.

Given WER measurements for several groups of speakers, we should also measure the *disparity* of the ASR performance across various groups. In a simplified way, one could calculate the difference between the best-performing and the worst-performing groups, but see Mitchell et al. (2020) for a general discussion of ML fairness metrics. While the WER gap in the best-group and the worst-performing group for the scenario depicted on the second subplot of Figure 1 is 3.5 absolute points, the gap is 12.8 absolute points for the distribution on the first subfigure—despite these two systems having the same average WER, one system is clearly more consistent than another.

Slicing can be based on just a single parameter, such as accent, gender, or age, but in reality, speakers are likely to fall into several categories at once. Therefore, it may make sense to look at *intersectional* groups: for example, ASR performance of 20-30 years old female speakers of Chicano English from Miami. Obtaining such rich metadata, however, may be challenging. Also, the more groups we intersect, the stronger the effect of data sparsity becomes: it may be challenging to fill every bucket with enough samples to obtain solid statistics and to control for all other variables not considered. At any rate, as long as mutually exclusive groups can be defined—whether based on a single parameter or in an intersectional way—this framework can help provide a more thorough understanding of various ASR metrics. Weighting by population also allows re-balancing potentially unbalanced test sets, and gives insight into what kinds of ASR performance would be encountered by different groups.

The goal of this approach is to generate new insights into the ASR accuracy for each slice without making assumptions about the causal interaction between the underlying latent variables. The analytical methods we discuss here are much more detailed than what is commonly employed for ASR system evaluation nowadays, but this level of detail is more usual in the field of variationist sociolinguistics, suggesting potential for future collaborations (Labov, 1990; Grama et al., 2019).

4.2 Defining slices

To evaluate the ASR systems in a framework that we are proposing, it is crucial to define representative and mutually exclusive slices. While the classification we suggest in this section is by no means exhaustive, it can be used as a starting point.

Regional language variation Many languages have regional language variation. For example, in the United States alone, there are 3 main regional groups of dialects: the Inland North, the South, and the West (Labov, 1991), with multiple cities developing their own regional language variants. Such regional variants may involve regional phonology ('get' rhymes with 'vet' in the North, and with 'fit' in the South), and even significant lexical and syntactic

[4]Top subplot: 6.5*0.6 + 13.9*0.3 + 19.3*0.1 = 10; bottom subplot: 8.9*0.6 + 11.4*0.3 + 12.4*0.1 = 10;

differences ('going/planning to' can be expressed as 'fixin' to' in the South). Aksënova et al. (2020) has shown how such regional variation can be explored, and how it can impact ASR performance. Ideally, then, as many regional variants as possible should be covered by the ideal benchmark for a given language.

Sociolects Along with regional differences, there may also also linguistic diversity introduced by speakers of various *sociolects*: in American English, one might think of AAVE, Chicano (Mexican-American) English, and others. For example, AAVE—covered by the CORAAL data set (Kendall and Farrington, 2020)—has distinctive syntactic constructions such as *habitual be* ('She be working') and *perfective done* ('He done run'), along with systematic phonological differences (Wolfram, 2004). And even within a single sociolect such as AAVE there might be linguistic diversity (Farrington et al., 2020). Sociolects may impact ASR quality (Koenecke et al., 2020), and it would therefore be desirable for benchmarks to cover as many sociolects as possible.

L2 background Speech produced by non-native (L2) may reflect some characteristics of their native (L1) language (Bloem et al., 2016), making it important to measure the impact of L2 accents on ASR accuracy. One relevant data set for English is the GMU Speech Accent Archive Weinberger (2015), which collects such data for L2 speakers of English.

Gender, age, and pitch Recognition performance may vary depending on the gender or age of the speaker (Liao et al., 2015; Tatman, 2017; Tatman and Kasten, 2017; Feng et al., 2021). In some cases, as in Common Voice (Ardila et al., 2020; Hazirbas et al., 2021), self-reported metadata is available. Where such information is not available, it may make sense to fall back to a proxy analysis based on pitch—which is known to be correlated with factors such as age and gender—in order to understand whether there are recognition accuracy differences for various pitch buckets, as in Liao et al. (2015).

Speech impairments Accuracy rates of standard ASR systems may also degrade for speech produced by people with speech impairments. Recent work has investigated ways to collect relevant data (Grill and Tučková, 2016; Park et al., 2021), enabling analyses of ASR systems in this area. However, given the high degree of variability in this space, a more robust path at least for the near-term future may be designing personalized ASR systems for people with non-standard speech (Shor et al., 2019). Beyond speech impairments, voice technologies could bring benefits to people with various types of diseases and impairments such as Alzheimer's, Parkinson's, and hearing loss.

5 Conclusion

The ultimate goal of benchmarking should be the ability to predict how well an ASR system is going to generalize to new and unseen data. In the previous sections we have argued that a single aggregate statistic like the average WER can be too coarse-grained for describing the accuracy in a real-world deployment that targets multiple sociolinguistic slices of the population. Ideally, the insights generated by the proposed analysis would be actionable, from the composition of the training data to fine-grained twiddling with a clear objective function.

Before we conclude, we should point out that any benchmark that implemented even a fraction of the metrics outlined above would yield rich amounts of information—which will likely pose challenges in terms of organizing, presenting, and understanding all this material. Model report cards, as outlined by Mitchell et al. (2019), may be a natural way to capture this information for an ASR system—although we would suggest calling them *system* report cards instead, given that most ASR systems do not consist solely of a single monolithic model. Given the sheer amount of variation in the ways in which people speak, and a large number of technical factors, measuring ASR systems is a complicated task. Today's benchmarks clearly leave room for improvement, whether it is through covering more horizontal domains (different kinds of speech), measuring the impact of cross-cutting vertical issues (e.g. factors like background noise), using more metrics than just WER (e.g. latency), and including demographic characteristics. We hope that our survey of these areas, and the simple population-weighted visualization framework we introduced, can help improve future benchmarks—not just for English, but also for the thousands of other languages spoken in our world today. This will clearly be a long-term journey, but it will be very important for the field as a whole to find ways to measure ASR systems better as speech recognition research continues to advance.

6 Acknowledgements

We thank our colleagues on the Google Speech team for many thoughtful discussions on this topic, especially Petar Aleksic, Geoff Fischer, Jonas Fromseier Mortensen, David Garcia, Millie Holt, Pedro J. Moreno, Pat Rondon, Benyah Shaparenko, and Eugene Weinstein.

References

Alëna Aksënova, Antoine Bruguier, Amanda Ritchart-Scott, and Uri Mendlovic. 2020. Algorithmic exploration of American English dialects. In *Proc. IEEE International Conference on Acoustics, Speech and Signal Processing (ICASSP)*, Barcelona, Spain.

Petar Aleksic, Mohammadreza Ghodsi, Assaf Michaely, Cyril Allauzen, Keith Hall, Brian Roark, David Rybach, and Pedro Moreno. 2015. Bringing contextual information to Google speech recognition. In *Proc. Interspeech 2015*, pages 468–472, Dresden, Germany.

McKane Andrus, Elena Spitzer, Jeffrey Brown, and Alice Xiang. 2021. What we can't measure, we can't understand: Challenges to demographic data procurement in the pursuit of fairness. In *Proc. ACM Conference on Fairness, Accountability, and Transparency*, page 249–260.

Ebrahim Ansari et al. 2020. Findings of the IWSLT 2020 evaluation campaign. In *Proc. International Conference on Spoken Language Translation*, pages 1–34.

Rosana Ardila, Megan Branson, Kelly Davis, Michael Kohler, Josh Meyer, Michael Henretty, Reuben Morais, Lindsay Saunders, Francis Tyers, and Gregor Weber. 2020. Common voice: A massively-multilingual speech corpus. In *Proc. Language Resources and Evaluation Conference*, pages 4218–4222, Marseille, France.

Mario Barcala, Eva Domínguez, Alba Fernández, Raquel Rivas, M. Paula Santalla, Victoria Vázquez, and Rebeca Villapol. 2018. El corpus ESLORA de español oral: diseño, desarrollo y explotación. *CHIMERA: Revista de Corpus de Lenguas Romances y Estudios Lingüísticos*, 5(2):217–237.

Fadi Biadsy, Mohammadreza Ghodsi, and Diamantino Caseiro. 2017. Effectively building tera scale maxent language models incorporating non-linguistic signals. In *Proc. Interspeech 2017*, pages 2710–2714, Stockholm, Sweden.

Douglas Biber. 1993. Representativeness in corpus design. *Literary and Linguistic Computing*, 8(4):243–257.

Jelke Bloem, Martijn Wieling, and John Nerbonne. 2016. *The Future of Dialects: Automatically identifying characteristic features of non-native English accents*, chapter 9. Language Science Press, Berlin, Germany.

Antoine Bruguier, Fuchun Peng, and Françoise Beaufays. 2016. Learning personalized pronunciations for contact name recognition. In *Proc. Interspeech 2016*, pages 3096–3100, San Francisco, CA, USA.

William Byrne, David Doermann, Martin Franz, Samuel Gustman, Jan Hajič, Douglas Oard, Michael Picheny, Josef Psutka, Bhuvana Ramabhadran, Dagobert Soergel, Todd Ward, and Wei-Jing Zhu. 2004. Automatic recognition of spontaneous speech for access to multilingual oral history archives. *IEEE Transactions on Speech and Audio Processing*, 12(4):420–435.

Alexandra Canavan, David Graff, and George Zipperlen. 1997. CALLHOME American English Speech LDC97S42. Web Download. Philadelphia: Linguistic Data Consortium.

Jean Carletta et al. 2005. The AMI meeting corpus: A pre-announcement. In *International Workshop on Machine Learning for Multimodal Interaction*, pages 28–39, Edinburgh, United Kingdom.

Nicholas Carlini and David Wagner. 2018. Audio adversarial examples: Targeted attacks on speech-to-text. In *IEEE Security and Privacy Workshops (SPW)*, pages 1–7, San Francisco, CA, USA.

Chung-Cheng Chiu, Anshuman Tripathi, Katherine Chou, Chris Co, Navdeep Jaitly, Diana Jaunzeikare, Anjuli Kannan, Patrick Nguyen, Hasim Sak, Ananth Sankar, Justin Tansuwan, Nathan Wan, Yonghui Wu, and Xuedong Zhang. 2018. Speech recognition for medical conversations. In *Proc. Interspeech 2018*, pages 2972–2976, Hyderabad, India.

Christopher Cieri, David Miller, and Kevin Walker. 2004. The Fisher corpus: a resource for the next generations of speech-to-text. In *Proc. International Conference on Language Resources and Evaluation*, pages 69–71, Lisbon, Portugal.

Ann Clifton, Sravana Reddy, Yongze Yu, Aasish Pappu, Rezvaneh Rezapour, Hamed Bonab, Maria Eskevich, Gareth Jones, Jussi Karlgren, Ben Carterette, and Rosie Jones. 2020. 100,000 podcasts: A spoken English document corpus. In *Proc. International Conference on Computational Linguistics*, pages 5903–5917, Barcelona, Spain.

Michelle Cohn, Melina Sarian, Kristin Predeck, and Georgia Zellou. 2020. Individual variation in language attitudes toward voice-AI: The role of listeners' autistic-like traits. In *Proc. Interspeech 2020*, pages 1813–1817, Shanghai, China.

Laura van Eerten. 2007. Over het corpus gesproken Nederlands. *Nederlandse Taalkunde*, 12(3):194–215.

Charlie Farrington, Sharese King, and Mary Kohn. 2020. Sources of variation in the speech of African Americans: Perspectives from sociophonetics. *WIREs Cognitive Science*, 12(3):1–17.

Siyuan Feng, Olya Kudina, Bence Mark Halpern, and Odette Scharenborg. 2021. Quantifying bias in automatic speech recognition. In *Proc. Interspeech 2021 (submitted)*, Brno, Czech Republic.

Eric Fosler-Lussier and Nelson Morgan. 1999. Effects of speaking rate and word frequency on pronunciations in conversational speech. *Speech Communication*, 29(2):137–158.

John S. Garofolo, Lori F. Lamel, William M. Fisher, Jonathan G. Fiscus, David S. Pallett, Nancy L. Dahlgren, and Victor Zue. 1993. TIMIT acoustic-phonetic continuous speech corpus LDC93S1. Web Download. Philadelphia: Linguistic Data Consortium.

Jort F. Gemmeke, Daniel P. W. Ellis, Dylan Freedman, Aren Jansen, Wade Lawrence, R. Channing Moore, Manoj Plakal, and Marvin Ritter. 2017. Audio Set: An ontology and human-labeled dataset for audio events. In *IEEE International Conference on Acoustics, Speech and Signal Processing (ICASSP)*, pages 776–780, New Orleans, LA, USA.

John J. Godfrey, Edward C. Holliman, and Jane McDaniel. 1992. SWITCHBOARD: Telephone speech corpus for research and development. In *IEEE International Conference on Acoustics, Speech, and Signal Processing (ICASSP)*, pages 517–520, San Francisco, CA, USA.

Christian Gollan, Maximilian Bisani, Stephan Kanthak, Ralf Schlüter, and Hermann Ney. 2005. Cross domain automatic transcription on the TC-STAR EPPS corpus. In *IEEE International Conference on Acoustics, Speech, and Signal Processing*, pages 825–828, Philadelphia, PA, USA.

James Grama, Catherine E. Travis, and Simon Gonzalez. 2019. Initiation, progression, and conditioning of the short-front vowel shift in Australia. In *Proc. International Congress of Phonetic Sciences (ICPhS)*, pages 1769–1773, Melbourne, Australia.

Pavel Grill and Jana Tučková. 2016. Speech databases of typical children and children with SLI. *PLOS ONE*, 11(3):1–21.

Isabelle Guyon, John Makhoul, Richard Schwartz, and Vladimir Vapnik. 1998. What size test set gives good error rate estimates? *IEEE Transactions on Pattern Analysis and Machine Intelligence*, 20(1):52–64.

Caner Hazirbas, Joanna Bitton, Brian Dolhansky, Jacqueline Pan, Albert Gordo, and Cristian Canton Ferrer. 2021. Towards measuring fairness in AI: the Casual Conversations dataset.

Rattaphon Hokking, Kuntpong Woraratpanya, and Yoshimitsu Kuroki. 2016. Speech recognition of different sampling rates using fractal code descriptor. In *Proc. International Joint Conference on Computer Science and Software Engineering (JCSSE)*, pages 1–5, Khon Kaen, Thailand.

Sara Hooker, Aaron Courville, Gregory Clark, Yann Dauphin, and Andrea Frome. 2020a. What do compressed deep neural networks forget?

Sara Hooker, Nyalleng Moorosi, Gregory Clark, Samy Bengio, and Emily Denton. 2020b. Characterising bias in compressed models. In *Proc. ICML Workshop on Human Interpretability in Machine Learning*.

Magdalena Igras-Cybulska, Bartosz Ziółko, Piotr Żelasko, and Marcin Witkowski. Structure of pauses in speech in the context of speaker verification and classification of speech type. *Journal on Audio, Speech, and Music Processing*, 2016(18):1–16.

Itorobong A. Inam, Ambrose A. Azeta, and Olawande Daramola. 2017. Comparative analysis and review of interactive voice response systems. In *Proc. Conference on Information Communication Technology and Society (ICTAS)*, pages 1–6, Durban, South Africa.

Paria Jamshid Lou and Mark Johnson. 2020. End-to-end speech recognition and disfluency removal. In *Findings of the Association for Computational Linguistics: EMNLP 2020*, pages 2051–2061.

Adam Janin, Jane Edwards, Dan Ellis, David Gelbart, Nelson Morgan, Barbara Peskin, Thilo Pfau, Elizabeth Shriberg, Andreas Stolcke, and Chuck Wooters. 2004. ICSI Meeting Speech LDC2004S02. Web Download. Philadelphia: Linguistic Data Consortium.

Naoyuki Kanda, Guoli Ye, Yu Wu, Yashesh Gaur, Xiaofei Wang, Zhong Meng, Zhuo Chen, and Takuya Yoshioka. 2021. Large-scale pre-training of end-to-end multi-talker ASR for meeting transcription with single distant microphone. In *Proc. Interspeech 2021 (submitted)*, Brno, Czech Republic.

Tyler Kendall and Charlie Farrington. 2020. The corpus of regional African American language. Version 2020.05. Eugene, OR: The Online Resources for African American Language Project.

Phillip Keung, Wei Niu, Yichao Lu, Julian Salazar, and Vikas Bhardwaj. 2020. Attentional speech recognition models misbehave on out-of-domain utterances.

Keisuke Kinoshita, Tsubasa Ochiai, Marc Delcroix, and Tomohiro Nakatani. 2020. Improving noise robust automatic speech recognition with single-channel time-domain enhancement network. In *IEEE International Conference on Acoustics, Speech and Signal Processing (ICASSP)*, pages 7009–7013, Barcelona, Spain.

Birgit Knudsen, Ava Creemers, and Antje S. Meyer. 2020. Forgotten little words: How backchannels and particles may facilitate speech planning in conversation? *Frontiers in Psychology*, 11:1–10.

Allison Koenecke, Andrew Nam, Emily Lake, Joe Nudell, Minnie Quartey, Zion Mengesha, Connor Toups, John R. Rickford, Dan Jurafsky, and Sharad Goel. 2020. Racial disparities in automated speech recognition. *Proc. of the National Academy of Sciences*, 117(14):7684–7689.

William Labov. 1990. The intersection of sex and social class in the course of linguistic change. *Language Variation and Change*, 2:205–254.

William Labov. 1991. The three dialects of English. In *New Ways of Analyzing Sound Change*, pages 1–44.

Vladimir Levenshtein. 1966. Binary codes capable of correcting deletions, insertions and reversals. *Soviet Physics Doklady*, 10:707.

Bo Li, Shuo-yiin Chang, Tara N. Sainath, Ruoming Pang, Yanzhang He, Trevor Strohman, and Yonghui Wu. 2020. Towards fast and accurate streaming end-to-end ASR. In *IEEE International Conference on Acoustics, Speech and Signal Processing (ICASSP)*, pages 6069–6073, Barcelona, Spain.

Hank Liao, Chris Alberti, Michiel Bacchiani, and Olivier Siohan. 2010. Decision tree state clustering with word and syllable features. In *Proc. Interspeech 2010*, page 2958 – 2961, Makuhari, Chiba, Japan.

Hank Liao, Golan Pundak, Olivier Siohan, Melissa Carroll, Noah Coccaro, Qi-Ming Jiang, Tara N. Sainath, Andrew Senior, Françoise Beaufays, and Michiel Bacchiani. 2015. Large vocabulary automatic speech recognition for children. In *Proc. Interspeech 2015*, pages 1611–1615, Dresden, Germany.

Tatiana Likhomanenko, Qiantong Xu, Vineel Pratap, Paden Tomasello, Jacob Kahn, Gilad Avidov, Ronan Collobert, and Gabriel Synnaeve. 2020. Rethinking evaluation in ASR: Are our models robust enough?

Jane W. S. Liu. 2000. *Real-time systems*. Prentice Hall, Upper Saddle River, NJ.

Anirudh Mani, Shruti Palaskar, and Sandeep Konam. 2020. Towards understanding ASR error correction for medical conversations. In *Proc. ACL 2020 Workshop on Natural Language Processing for Medical Conversations*, pages 7–11.

Peter Mattson et al. 2020. MLPerf training benchmark. In *Proc. Conference on Machine Learning and Systems*, pages 1–14, Austin, TX, USA.

Shannon McCrocklin. 2019. ASR-based dictation practice for second language pronunciation improvement. *Journal of Second Language Pronunciation*, 5(1):98–118.

Valentin Mendelev, Tina Raissi, Guglielmo Camporese, and Manuel Giollo. 2021. Improved robustness to disfluencies in RNN-Transducer based speech recognition. In *IEEE International Conference on Acoustics, Speech and Signal Processing (ICASSP)*, Toronto, Canada.

Adam S. Miner, Albert Haque, Jason Alan Fries, Scott L. Fleming, Denise E. Wilfley, G. Terence Wilson, Arnold Milstein, Dan Jurafsky, Bruce A. Arnow, W. Stewart Agras, Li Fei-Fei, and Nigam H. Shah. 2020. Assessing the accuracy of automatic speech recognition for psychotherapy. *npj Digital Medicine*, 3(82).

Margaret Mitchell, Dylan Baker, Nyalleng Moorosi, Emily Denton, Ben Hutchinson, Alex Hanna, Timnit Gebru, and Jamie Morgenstern. 2020. Diversity and inclusion metrics in subset selection. In *Proc. AAAI/ACM Conference on AI, Ethics, and Society*, page 117–123, New York, NY, USA.

Margaret Mitchell, Simone Wu, Andrew Zaldivar, Parker Barnes, Lucy Vasserman, Ben Hutchinson, Elena Spitzer, Inioluwa Deborah Raji, and Timnit Gebru. 2019. Model cards for model reporting. In *Proc. Conference on Fairness, Accountability, and Transparency*, page 220–229, Atlanta, GA, USA.

Patrick K. O'Neill, Vitaly Lavrukhin, Somshubra Majumdar, Vahid Noroozi, Yuekai Zhang, Oleksii Kuchaiev, Jagadeesh Balam, Yuliya Dovzhenko, Keenan Freyberg, Michael D. Shulman, Boris Ginsburg, Shinji Watanabe, and Georg Kucsko. 2021. SPGISpeech: 5,000 hours of transcribed financial audio for fully formatted end-to-end speech recognition. In *Proc. Interspeech 2021 (submitted)*, Brno, Czech Republic.

Mukund Padmanabhan, George Saon, Jing Huang, Brian Kingsbury, and Lidia Mangu. 2002. Automatic speech recognition performance on a voicemail transcription task. *IEEE Transactions on Speech and Audio Processing*, 10(7):433–442.

Vassil Panayotov, Guoguo Chen, Daniel Povey, and Sanjeev Khudanpur. 2015. Librispeech: An ASR corpus based on public domain audio books. In *IEEE International Conference on Acoustics, Speech and Signal Processing (ICASSP)*, pages 5206–5210, South Brisbane, Australia.

Naveen Parihar and Joseph Picone. 2002. Aurora Working Group: DSR Front End LVCSR Evaluation AU/384/02. Technical report, Mississippi State University.

Daniel S. Park, William Chan, Yu Zhang, Chung-Cheng Chiu, Barret Zoph, Ekin D. Cubuk, and Quoc V. Le. 2019. SpecAugment: A simple data augmentation method for automatic speech recognition. In *Proc. Interspeech 2019*, pages 2613–2617, Graz, Austria.

Joon Sung Park, Danielle Bragg, Ece Kamar, and Meredith Ringel Morris. 2021. Designing an online infrastructure for collecting AI data from people with disabilities. In *Proc. ACM Conference on Fairness, Accountability, and Transparency*, page 52–63.

Douglas B. Paul and Janet M. Baker. 1992. The design for the Wall Street Journal-based CSR corpus. In *Speech and Natural Language: Proceedings of a Workshop Held at Harriman, New York, February 23-26, 1992*.

David Pearce and Hans-Günter Hirsch. 2000. The AURORA experimental framework for the performance evaluations of speech recognition systems under noisy condition. In *Proc. International Conference on Spoken Language Processing*, pages 29–32, Beijing, China.

Zilun Peng, Akshay Budhkar, Ilana Tuil, Jason Levy, Parinaz Sobhani, Raphael Cohen, and Jumana Nassour. 2021. Shrinking Bigfoot: Reducing wav2vec 2.0 footprint. In *Proc. Interspeech 2021 (submitted)*, Brno, Czech Republic.

Cal Peyser, Hao Zhang, Tara N. Sainath, and Zelin Wu. 2019. Improving performance of end-to-end ASR on numeric sequences. In *Proc. Interspeech 2019*, pages 2185–2189, Graz, Austria.

Andrew Rosenberg. 2012. Rethinking the corpus: Moving towards dynamic linguistic resources. In *Proc. Interspeech 2012*, pages 1392–1395, Portland, OR, USA.

Neville Ryant, Prachi Singh, Venkat Krishnamohan, Rajat Varma, Kenneth Church, Christopher Cieri, Jun Du, Sriram Ganapathy, and Mark Liberman. 2021. The third DIHARD diarization challenge.

Tara N. Sainath, Ruoming Pang, David Rybach, Basi García, and Trevor Strohman. 2020a. Emitting word timings with end-to-end models. In *Proc. Interspeech 2020*, pages 3615–3619, Shanghai, China.

Tara N. Sainath et al. 2020b. A streaming on-device end-to-end model surpassing server-side conventional model quality and latency. In *IEEE International Conference on Acoustics, Speech and Signal Processing (ICASSP)*, pages 6059–6063, Barcelona, Spain.

Conrad Sanderson and Kuldip K. Paliwal. 1997. Effect of different sampling rates and feature vector sizes on speech recognition performance. In *IEEE Speech and Image Technologies for Computing and Telecommunications*, volume 1, pages 161–164.

George Saon, Gakuto Kurata, Tom Sercu, Kartik Audhkhasi, Samuel Thomas, Dimitrios Dimitriadis, Xiaodong Cui, Bhuvana Ramabhadran, Michael Picheny, Lynn-Li Lim, Bergul Roomi, and Phil Hall. 2017. English conversational telephone speech recognition by humans and machines. In *Proc. Interspeech 2017*, pages 132–136, Stockholm, Sweden.

Yuan Shangguan, Kate Knister, Yanzhang He, Ian McGraw, and Françoise Beaufays. 2020. Analyzing the quality and stability of a streaming end-to-end on-device speech recognizer. In *Proc. Interspeech 2020*, pages 591–595, Shanghai, China.

Yuan Shangguan, Rohit Prabhavalkar, Hang Su, Jay Mahadeokar, Yangyang Shi, Jiatong Zhou, Chunyang Wu, Duc Le, Ozlem Kalinli, Christian Fuegen, and Michael L. Seltzer. 2021. Dissecting user-perceived latency of on-device E2E speech recognition. In *Proc. Interspeech 2021 (submitted)*, Brno, Czech Republic.

Joel Shor, Dotan Emanuel, Oran Lang, Omry Tuval, Michael Brenner, Julie Cattiau, Fernando Vieira, Maeve McNally, Taylor Charbonneau, Melissa Nollstadt, Avinatan Hassidim, and Yossi Matias. 2019. Personalizing ASR for dysarthric and accented speech with limited data. In *Proc. Interspeech 2019*, pages 784–788, Graz, Austria.

Matthew A. Siegler and Richard M. Stern. 1995. On the effects of speech rate in large vocabulary speech recognition systems. In *IEEE International Conference on Acoustics, Speech, and Signal Processing (ICASSP)*, pages 612–615, Detroit, MI, USA.

Richard Sproat, Alan W. Black, Stanley Chen, Shankar Kumar, Mari Ostendorf, and Christopher Richards. 2001. Normalization of non-standard words. *Computer Speech & Language*, 15(3):287–333.

Steintór Steingrímsson, Starkadur Barkarson, and Gunnar Thor Örnólfsson. 2020. IGC-parl: Icelandic corpus of parliamentary proceedings. In *Proc. ParlaCLARIN Workshop*, pages 11–17, Marseille, France.

Piotr Szymański, Piotr Żelasko, Mikolaj Morzy, Adrian Szymczak, Marzena Żyła-Hoppe, Joanna Banaszczak, Lukasz Augustyniak, Jan Mizgajski, and Yishay Carmiel. 2020. WER we are and WER we think we are. In *Findings of the Association for Computational Linguistics: EMNLP 2020*, pages 3290–3295.

Rachael Tatman. 2017. Gender and dialect bias in YouTube's automatic captions. In *Proc. ACL Workshop on Ethics in Natural Language Processing*, pages 53–59, Valencia, Spain.

Rachael Tatman and Conner Kasten. 2017. Effects of talker dialect, gender & race on accuracy of Bing Speech and YouTube automatic captions. In *Proc. Interspeech 2017*, pages 934–938, Stockholm, Sweden.

Ye-Yi Wang, Alex Acero, and Ciprian Chelba. 2003. Is word error rate a good indicator for spoken language understanding accuracy. In *IEEE Workshop on Automatic Speech Recognition and Understanding*, pages 577–582, St Thomas, VI, USA.

Steven Weinberger. 2015. Speech accent archive. George Mason University.

Walt Wolfram. 2004. *Handbook of varieties of English: The grammar of urban African American Vernacular English*, pages 111–132. Mouton de Gruyter, Berlin, Germany.

Wayne Xiong, Jasha Droppo, Xuedong Huang, Frank Seide, Michael L. Seltzer, Andreas Stolcke, Dong Yu, and Geoffrey Zweig. 2017. Toward human parity in conversational speech recognition. *IEEE/ACM Transactions on Audio, Speech, and Language Processing*, 25(12):2410–2423.

Dong Yu, Jinyu Li, and Li Deng. 2011. Calibration of confidence measures in speech recognition. *IEEE Transactions on Audio, Speech, and Language Processing*, 19(8):2461–2473.

Jiahui Yu, Chung-Cheng Chiu, Bo Li, Shuo-yiin Chang, Tara N. Sainath, Yanzhang (Ryan) He, Arun Narayanan, Wei Han, Anmol Gulati, Yonghui Wu, and Ruoming Pang. 2021. FastEmit: Low-latency streaming ASR with sequence-level emission regularization. In *IEEE International Conference on Acoustics, Speech and Signal Processing (ICASSP)*, Toronto, Canada.

Yu Zhang, James Qin, Daniel S. Park, Wei Han, Chung-Cheng Chiu, Ruoming Pang, Quoc V. Le, and Yonghui Wu. 2020. Pushing the limits of semi-supervised learning for automatic speech recognition. In *Proc. NeurIPS Workshop on Self-Supervised Learning for Speech and Audio Processing*.

Author Index